A SCRIBNERS BOOK

First published in Great Britain in 1990 by Scribners
a Division of Macdonald & Co (Publishers) Ltd
London & Sydeny

British Library Cataloguing in Publication data
The Sheltering Sky: a film by Bernardo Bertolucci
based on the novel by Paul Bowles.
1. Cinema films. Production 791.430232

ISBN 0-356-19579-1

Printed and bound in Verona, Italy, by ARTEGRAFICA
Photo scanning by INTEGRAL GRAPHIC - Paris

Scribners
A Division of Macdonald & Co. (Publishers) Ltd.
Orbit House, 1 New Fetter Lane, London EC4A 1AR

A member of Maxwell Macmillan Pergamon Publishing Corporation plc.

◆

Book devised, edited and produced by **LIVIO NEGRI**
Co-editor **FABIEN S. GERARD**
Graphic design **RAMPAZZO & ASSOCIÉS** - Paris
Photo cover by **ANGELO NOVI**
Photographs by **ANGELO NOVI** and **FABIAN CEVALLOS**
Additional photographs by **FABIEN S. GERARD, GIORGIO LOTTI**
Consultant **WARWICK HEMBRY**
Drawing **RENE' F. FOLLET**
Mock-up **LAURENCE LE PIOUFF**
Execution **NATA RAMPAZZO & DINO MAZZOLA** - Editorial Service
Texts Revisions **PARISSA NAHANI, SEVILLA DELOFSKI**
Facilities **HAPPY VALLEY FILMS Ltd.**

Contributors (in alphabetical order)

JAMES ACHESON	WILLIAM ALDRICH
GEORGES-LOUIS BOURGEOIS	PAUL BOWLES
ROBERT BRIATTE	GABRIELLA CRISTIANI
MILLICENT DILLON	FABIEN S. GERARD
RICHARD HOROWITZ	RENATO LEYS
MARK PEPLOE	RYUICHI SAKAMOTO
GIANNI SILVESTRI	VITTORIO STORARO
JEREMY THOMAS	FABIO TRONCARELLI
DEBRA WINGER	

Translations
Eugene Rizzo, Jane Dunnitt

Photo Archive
Cecil Beaton, Karl Bissinger, Marcus Blachman, Paul Bowles, British Film Institute, Cahiers du Cinéma,
Cinêmathèque de Bruxelles, Tessa Codrington, Photography Collection at the Harry Ransom Humanities
Research Center at the University of Texas at Austin, Suzanne Durrenberger, Gerard Gastaud, Hugh Gibb, Allen
Ginsberg, Kobal Collection, Mary Allen Mark, Angelo Novi, The Oscar Reinhart Foundation of Winterthur,
Popperfoto, Terence Spencer

Special thanks
Bernardo Bertolucci, Jeremy Thomas, Tilde Corsi, Debra Winger, John Malkovich, Nata Rampazzo, Fabian
Cevallos, Hercules Belville, Caty Henderson, Cary Thorton, Ly Bryks, Paul Bowles, Catherine MacKenzie, Monique
Kouznetzoff and Beatrice Wachsberger/Sygma, Zoe McCrudden and Caroline Taylor/Corbett & Keene Ltd.,
Robert Briatte, Julia Bunton, Peter G. Brown, Clare Peploe, July Oudot, Luana Chambers/ICA Entertainment,
Vincent Dandoy, Jean-Paul Dorchain, Tim Adler, Christiane Montulet, Oliver Krimpas, Odile Nass, Ann Tasker,
Brice Mattheuson, Lizzie Franke, Veronique Gerard-Powell, Jacques Cormier, Jean-Marc Spiller, Carolyn Harms,
Julian Dickens, Julie Derbyshire, Ron Swinburne, Daniel Davids/Glinwood Films, Mia/Creative Partnership,
Jocelyn Cousins, Françoise Michaux, Valentine Bertrand

JEREMY THOMAS PRESENTS A BERNARDO BERTOLUCCI FILM

The Sheltering Sky

BASED ON THE NOVEL BY PAUL BOWLES

Book devised, edited and produced by
LIVIO NEGRI

Co-editor
FABIEN S. GERARD

Graphic design
RAMPAZZO & ASSOCIÉS-Paris

Photographs
ANGELO NOVI and **FABIAN CEVALLOS**

Scribners

C O N T E N T S

PAUL BOWLES
with BERNARDO
BERTOLUCCI

When I realized that I was being photographed in the same scene with my two protagonists Port and Kit, I thought: *'What am I doing here? I have no right to be here. I don't exist. I'm spoiling the scene with my presence.'*

▶ Not having seen any rushes, and thus having no idea of the general aspect of the film, I can only imagine, and not know, what it would be like to look down the long corridor of time into the past, and see the places and events which have existed only in my mind come into being before my eyes. I can imagine it, and it seems to me that it ought to be a satisfying sensation (although involvement with the distant past can easily slip into something more painful than pleasant).

▶ The reason for my confused reaction to finding myself before the camera was that I had no idea why I had been put there. Undoubtedly Bertolucci had explained it all to me, but I had failed to understand the reason for my being included in that café scene at the opening of the film.

▶ The film begins. The characters about to appear and the actions about to follow first existed in the mind of this man a good many years ago. Now he is seeing these ideas transmuted into the image of human beings with faces and bodies, watching them set out on their doomed journey, even wishing vaguely that there was some way of warning them. But to do that, he would first have to exist. If that were possible, and he did, the warning would have no effect; the trip must be made because he originally determined that they must make it. They are programmed to do so; this programming is their essence. It is no consolation for him to say that they do not exist. He has planned their suffering, and now they do exist. It is he who does not.

▶ Once I understood the purpose served by my being there, I realized that it was a brilliant conceit of my director's to show the author in the act of viewing his protagonists as they perform the gestures he devised for them. It's not often that a writer has that privilege.

Tangier, April 1990

Paul Bowles

The Sheltering Sky

A PORTRAIT OF THE FILM

◆

1947. An ocean liner from New York sets Kit and Port Moresby down in TANGIER. They are seasoned adventurers with no plans to return. Their friend Tunner wants to return with snapshots and stories of sexual conquests. He is a tourist. They are travellers.

◆

◆

Port's dream is to take the three of them across the Sahara and seek inspiration for his music in distant lands.

Kit wrote her first play years ago. Unable to complete a further work, she now feverishly fills her journal whilst pushing aside Tunner's advances.

◆

◆

The restless Port prowls in the night following the distant drums to the city's edge where a nomad girl entertains him in a tent. The drums stop and, in the sudden silence, he awakes to find the girl's body entwined around him and his life in danger.

◆

The Lyles, a monstrous mother and son, avidly watch every move the three Americans make. The eccentric Mrs Lyle is a travel guides' writer. Her son, Eric, acts as her chauffeur. They find that the Moresby's journey coincides with theirs, and issue an invitation that is impossible to evade.

There is room for Kit in the Lyles' white Mercedes, but her sense of friendship will not allow her to leave Tunner to travel alone, and she chooses to accompany him on the train. With the magic of champagne, Tunner succeeds in breaking down Kit's reserve.

◆

The small group reunites in BOUSSIF, where Port seizes an opportunty to be alone with Kit. On the top of the ridge, they find their own solitary place.

◆

A hellish swarm of flies greets the travellers in AIN KRORFA. Port insists that it is Tunner's turn to take advantage of the Lyles' car which will go directly to Messad, where they will all meet later.

◆

Arriving in BOU NOURA, the couple are now left to themselves. Soon the broken pieces of their ten year marriage surface and overwhelm them. Port seeks oblivion at a feast in the local brothel.

◆

◆

Next stop is EL GA'A. Getting off the bus, Port collapses, overcome by fever. A young Arab leads Kit to the only hotel where she is met by a closed door and told to leave immediately — there is a typhoid epidemic raging in the area. Once more, they are forced to go deeper into the desert.

◆

T H E . F I L M

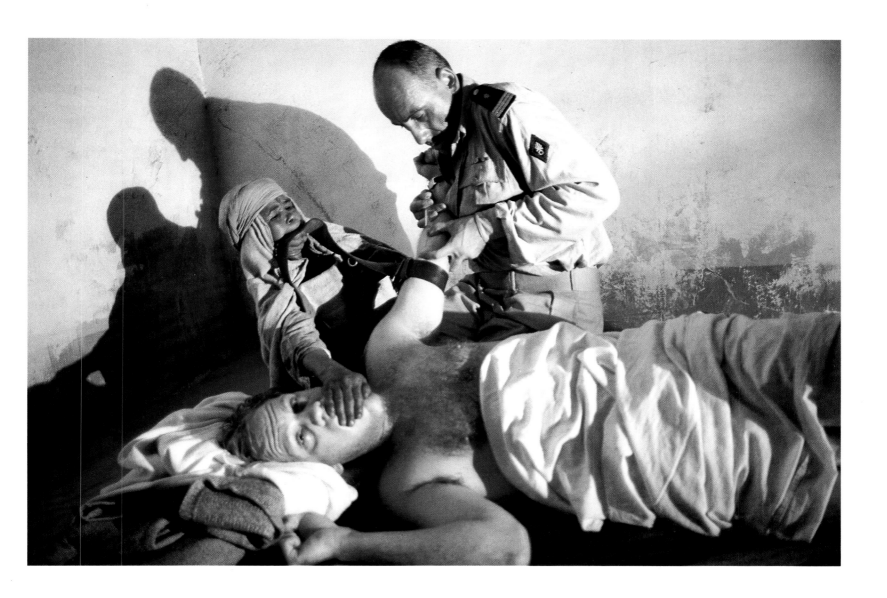

◆

FORT SBA is the last point of civilization. The captain of the fort provides medicines that prove to be useless. With diminishing hope, Kit keeps her vigil at Port's side, attempting to submerge her fear in the daily rituals of nursing. By the time Tunner finally catches up with them, Port has died.

◆

◆

Twilight. Kit leaves Port's body alone and immerses herself in a pool at the heart of the palmgrove. At dawn a caravan of camel traders, the fabled 'Blue-Men' of the Sahara, comes into view. She regains control and demands to ride with them. Sitting behind a young Tuareg nomad, Belqassim, she disappears into the dunes.

◆

◆

After crossing the vast ocean of sand, Kit finds herself alone with her innermost feelings and enclosed in her own sensual world. Disguised as an Arab boy in an attempt to fool Belqassim's wives, she eats, sleeps and thirsts for her Tuareg's secret visits. One morning, during his absence, the deception is exposed.

◆

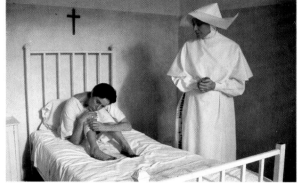

◆

TANGIER, some weeks later. Kit has been rescued and placed in a hospital. Tunner, who has continued to search for her, is told that she has returned, but Kit, unable to meet him, disappears again into the labyrinth of the Medina. There, she sees in her path an elderly gentleman who seems strangely familiar to her. His name is Paul Bowles.

◆

The Territories of the Sky

BY ROBERT BRIATTE

'**Y**ou're going to Tangier? In that case you ought to call on Paul Bowles, — that's what people say in New York. They turn up but they have nothing to say to me and I have nothing to say to them,' says Paul Bowles. 'They arrive, then they leave. There's not much to see in Tangier, you understand. I'm a sort of monument to be visited along the way. I don't know why they come here, nor do they, so they end up by asking me why I came here... I didn't choose to live in Tangier. It just happened.' [1]

PAUL at the age of four.
'I had an extraordinarily uneventful early childhood; only my imagination made it bearable, substituting fantasy for reality.'

▶ Paul Bowles was born on December 30, 1910 in Long Island. A medium, consulted at his birth, foresaw 'piles of paper' strewn around the child. The medium was an idea of his mother, who, from his second birthday, would read to him every evening stories from Edgar Allan Poe's *Tales of Mystery and Imagination*. A lonely child in an exclusively adult world — it was not until he began attending school that he would encounter children his own age — Paul soon came to understand that for his parents '*whatever is forbidden is the supreme virtue*' and that he should do everything in his power to protect his inner life. '*I became an expert in the practice of deceit, at least insofar as general mien and facial expressions were concerned. I could not make myself lie, inasmuch as for me the word and its literal meaning had supreme importance, but I could feign enthusiasm for what I disliked, and even more essential, hide whatever enjoyment I felt.*' [2]

▶ At the age of five Paul completed his own first work of fiction, a short story about animals; at eight Paul was taking regular piano lessons: yet his greatest love was for improvisation. '*When I was a child, I preferred my own music to other people's. That was the reason I decided I'd be a composer.*' Before meeting with the rising musician Aaron Copland, the future composer of such ballets as *Billy the Kid* and *Appalachian Spring*, who was going to teach him the technique of composition, Paul Bowles dabbled in painting, applied himself to the technique of automatic writing and published a handful of surrealist poems in the Parisian review *Transition*. In March 1929 he interrupted his studies in the middle of the very first year at college and booked his passage to France. While his parents were having him traced across the United States, he arrived in Paris with precisely twenty-four dollars to his name. For the first time in his life he had broken from the prison that America represented to him. Bowles returned to New York after five months' escape. His resolve to become a composer was unchanged and he began studying with Copland. In the spring of 1931 Bowles set off with Copland for Berlin. Somewhere, however, between Paris and Salzburg, Paul realized that he was more at ease as a collector of celebrities than as the attentive disciple of a single master. To his collection he would add such prize specimens as Gertrude Stein and Alice B. Toklas, Jean Cocteau, Gide, Ezra Pound, Kurt Schwitters, Krishnamurti, Walter Gropius, and many others.

▶ It was Gertrude Stein who discouraged him from writing poetry. '*I showed her my poems. She read them and said: They are fine. The only problem is that's not poetry*'. It was also Gertrude Stein who dispatched the student and his music master to a holiday in Tangier where he completed his first major work, a *Sonata for Oboe and Clarinet*. What Morocco presented him with was a wonderful, uninterrupted soundtrack, and its inhabitants were to become the spontaneous and unrehearsed actors of a permanent show. '*I had based my sense of being in the world partly on an unreasoned conviction that certain areas of the earth's surface contained more magic than others. Had anyone asked me what I mean by magic, I should probably have defined the word by calling it a secret connection between the world of nature and the consciousness of man, a hidden but direct passage which by-passed the mind.*' [3]

▶ From that moment on he would conjugate the verb to travel in every possible tense. For the year 1931 alone he had twelve different addresses. One year later he explored Algeria and crossed the Sahara. It was this first memory that would provide the setting for *The Sheltering Sky*, the account of a one-way trip

GERTRUDE STEIN: 'You must go to Tangier!' — 'No one would say no to Gertrude.'

JANE BOWLES, 1954.
'There were times she believed she was the best writer in the world. Then she'd say: Everything I've done is shit!'

undertaken by a fictional self towards the desert, towards the territories of the sky and of oblivion. '*Here, in this wholly mineral landscape, lighted by the stars like flares, even memory disappears; nothing is left but your own breathing and the sound of your heart beating. A strange, and by no means pleasant , process of reintegration begins inside you, and it remains to be seen whether you will fight against it, and insist on remaining the person you have always been, or whether you will let it take its course. For no one who has stayed in the Sahara for a while is quite the same as when he came.*' [4]

▶ After a last trip to Tangier in 1934, Paul Bowles spent the next thirteen years concentrating on music while travelling mostly in Central America till the end of the Second World War. He earned his living by composing ballets, soundtrack scores for numerous films and incidental music for Broadway plays staged by personalities as diverse as George Balanchine, Orson Welles, Salvador Dali, José Ferrer and Elia Kazan. He collaborated with several of the period's best-known dramatists - Arthur Koestler, Lillian Hellman and William Saroyan. For John Huston he translated Sartre's *No Exit* and composed incidental music for four of the most famous of Tennessee Williams' plays. Such commissions, however, could not deter him from creating a more personal body of work: fourteen compositions for piano and orchestra, three compositions for voice and three operas.

▶ In February 1937, during an evening spent smoking marijuana in Harlem, Paul met Jane Auer, a young habituée of the clubs and literary drawing-rooms of Manhattan, a pillar of 'Café Society' possessed of an extraordinarily seductive and original personality, both unpredictable and generous. Jane was above all else determined to be a writer. Paul initially struck her as a rather sinister figure and she confided to a woman friend 'That man is my enemy.' A few days later, nevertheless, they left for Mexico; and subsequently parted, the previous animosity having caught up with them. Finally, on February 21, 1938, on the eve of her twenty-first birthday, Jane was to become Mrs Bowles. The couple set forth on a lengthy honeymoon encompassing, first, a number of central American countries, then France. '*Jane and I would always speak French together. Having lived a long time in Europe, she'd grown accustomed to speaking and thinking in French. In 1935-36, she wrote her first novel in French* Le Phaéton Hypocrite. *It's been lost. Not a single copy exists. But she did that deliberately. She tried to do exactly the same thing with her collection of short stories* Plain Pleasures. *She would always want to destroy everything she did. Why? I've no idea. There were times she believed she was the best writer in the world. Then she'd say "Everything I've done is shit!" She was a psychological mystery.*'

TANGIER, 1930. *'Certainly I never expected that I would end my life holed up in a place like Tangier.'*

▶ On a May night in 1947 Paul Bowles dreamt of Tangier. It was a long time since he had visited the 'white city'. In the labyrinth of the unconscious the images of his dreams delineated a landscape of quite startling precision: narrow little alleys designed to make one lose one's way, terraces looking out over the ocean, staircases ascending nowhere. He decided to spend the summer in Morocco — a cloudless summer, one lived as close as possible to the sky, for as he knew, in order to write a novel, he would have to be alone. He left Jane behind in the United States, where she was working on her first play In the Summer House. That August in Fez he began writing The Sheltering Sky, a title he had arrived at before departing from New York, during the ten minute bus journey from 10th Street to Madison Square Gardens when he had also plotted out its narrative. The title derives from a popular pre-First World War song, Down Among the Sheltering Palms. A spellbound Paul had often listened to it on his grandfather's phonographs. 'It was not the banal melody which fascinated me, but the strange word "sheltering". What did the palm trees shelter people from, and how sure could they be of such protection?'

▶ Paul Bowles never fully recovered from reading the Hiroshima headline one August morning in 1945. It is, even now, his conviction that *'there is no protection or security anywhere.'* By returning to Morocco on the prompting of a dream, he was not only withdrawing from the world in order to write a novel but fleeing a bellicose and imperialist land, the America of John Wayne. Similarly, his protagonists flee those continents where the war has left too many traces; they abandon a world in which they no longer recognise themselves. The idea of remaining in this self-styled civilization has become intolerable to them, as it would imply their complicity in what is happening to it.

▶ The themes addressed by *The Sheltering Sky* are of profound concern to each and every one of us: the loss of illusions, the impossibility of mutual understanding, the death of love... In the immediate aftermath of the Second World War, with the long chapter of decolonization just beginning, Africa alone held out the hopes of a new continent. The Sahara could still serve as a backdrop to the kind of radical self-interrogation to which Port and Kit Moresby subject themselves. The distinctive feature of the landscapes in which Bowles' protagonists move and evolve is that nothing exists in the desert to protect us from the sun's dazzling severity, nothing exists to distinguish us from the stones, from the very grains of sand, at our feet. The territories of the sky compose a terrain favourable to revelation, a vast open space in which the truth

PAUL BOWLES, Tangier, 1963.
'My life consists of the places where I have lived and the work I have accomplished in those places.'

'From the thirties through the sixties living in Tangier was predicated upon the ease with which one could sail to any part of the world.'

Vue Panoramique du Grand Soko.

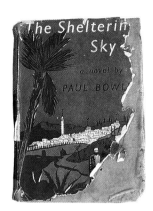

THE SHELTERING SKY, 1949.

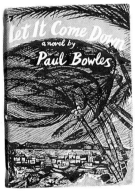

LET IT COME DOWN, 1952.

of the human condition is finally, mercilessly, exposed. And when it opens up, what it offers us is no more than the certitude of nothingness. '*His cry went on through the final image: the spots of raw bright blood on the earth. Blood on excrement. The supreme moment, high above the desert, when the two elements, blood and excrement, long kept apart, merge. A black star appears, a point of darkness in the night sky's clarity. Point of darkness and gateway to repose. Reach out, pierce the fine fabric of the sheltering sky, take repose.*' [5]

❱ It is at the very moment when she realises that Port is dead that Kit at last is free. Free to leave, free to forge a path to her own oblivion. '*From a certain point onward there is no longer any turning back. That is the point that must be reached.*' [6]

❱ Paul Bowles is a writer of unease, each of whose books deals with the end or loss of something. His first novel, *The Sheltering Sky*, of an astonishing bleakness and maturity, shared with a short story that he had just published, *A Distant Episode*, the theme of loss of identity; and in the way it amplifies such a theme, *The Sheltering Sky* recorded the end of the whole sentimental illusion that the desert had long inspired. His following novels, *Let it Come Down* and *The Spider's House*, are set at historical turning points, with chaos about to break loose on humanity. In *Up Above the World* the brutal death of yet another couple is detailed with characteristic detachment. The landscape itself seems fated to be destroyed and the only hope remaining — in the abstract perception of beauty — soon completely evaporates.

❱ Bowles does not regard himself as a guru. He simply has the impression of having arrived on the scene in time to be present at the end of a certain conception of nature and the world. But, with him, the realisation that such an outcome is inevitable is transformed into a serene acceptance of life, an almost tranquil sense of resignation. Fear is present, latent in the very core of being and there is nothing to do but acknowledge it. He has come to accept that the world will end with an attenuated whimper rather than a bang. The fragmentation and disjunction of the world, and the diminished expectations we have of it, this we can all acknowledge: it is up to each of us to discover our own form of self-preservation. In fact, Paul Bowles is without expectations — which leaves him curiously open and accessible. He does not judge: he writes. And if he writes, it is to satisfy, against all odds, a need for form, a need to lend aesthetic meaning to existence.

PAUL BOWLES, 1985. '*In my tale there are no dramatic victories because there was no struggle. I hung on and waited. It seems to me that this must be what most people do.*'

▶ After *The Sheltering Sky* he embarked upon a new life. He gradually abandoned composition and started to devote himself exclusively to the written word. In 1953, he was asked by the Italian film director Luchino Visconti to write the dialogue of *Senso*, but Tennessee Williams had to rewrite the film's love scenes, which the director found *'too cold'*. In the previous year he had acquired Taprobane, an idyllic isle off the coast of Ceylon where he was to write the major part of *The Spider's House*. In 1957 he at least completed, a whole decade after having begun it, the composition of his second opera, *Yerma*, from Lorca's play. And it was in that same year that Jane fell gravely ill from a cerebral haemorrhage. Nothing would ever be the same again. It was as though life had come to a halt for her. She died in 1973 in a psychiatric clinic in Malaga, having only ever published one novel, one stage play, and one collection of short stories. *'Her death was a terrible ordeal'*, says Bowles, *'as it was half of myself that I lost. I no longer wanted to do anything at all.'*

▶ These days Paul Bowles writes very little. *'You have to be severe with books'* he says, *'since they're all that remain.'* It is my belief that he has never sought to do anything else as an artist than invite us to accompany him into a universe measuring up to both his nightmares and our own. He is prepared to keep his door ajar to anyone who wishes to cross its threshold. However, he takes good care to leave all truly personal questions unanswered. And the answers one thinks one has received are such that they only beg further questions.

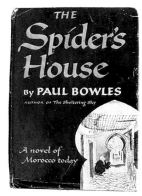

THE SPIDER'S HOUSE, 1955.

UP ABOVE THE WORLD, 1966.

NOTES:
(1) R.Briatte, PAUL BOWLES, Editions Plon, Paris, 1989, p.11
(2) P.Bowles, WITHOUT STOPPING, Hamish Hamilton, 1989, p.17
(3) WITHOUT STOPPING, cit., p.125
(4): P.Bowles, THEIR HEADS ARE GREEN, Abacus, 1990, p.119
(5) P.Bowles, THE SHELTERING SKY, Grafton Books, 1986, p.245
(6) A quotation from Kafka in THE SHELTERING SKY, cit., p.277

ROBERT BRIATTE, is the author of the only authorized biography on Paul Bowles (*Paul Bowles*, Plon, 1989). Other titles include *Joseph Delteil* (1988) and a book on Tangier, where he has lived for two years, *Tanger s'il y a Lieu*, (1988). Robert Briatte is responsible for having introduced in 1986 the music of Paul Bowles in France with several radio programmes for France Culture.

What Happened to Kit?

AN INTERVIEW BY FABIO TRONCARELLI

BOWLES: The life of a writer has no interest; what he likes or does has no importance. There can be a relation between life and work, but that is just a supposition. I hope I will disappear without having told the depth of my thinking. You can find the depth of my thinking in my writing and in my music.

How did you go from music to writing?

BOWLES: At first I was working as a composer, I felt like a musician and I was content until I began to realize there were feelings I couldn't put into music. What I discovered was that I couldn't express with music the negative side of myself which instead I was able to paint with words. I wrote a short story, *Tea on the Mountain*, in 1939, but then there was nothing until 1945 when I wrote *A Distant Episode*. By 1947 I had written a fair number of short stories, enough for a book. I gave them to a publisher, but his reply was that no one could start as a short story writer and that I had to begin with a novel. I got in touch with a literary agent, Helen Strauss of William Morris, and she obtained a contract for me with Doubleday.

Did Jane play any part in the writing of your novels?

BOWLES: I wouldn't have started writing if I hadn't been married to Jane... yes; if I hadn't lived with her and been caught up in the writing of her novel *Two Serious Ladies*. It was while reading her novel, discussing it with her, that I felt I wanted to write too.

Did you use any particular method of writing for *The Sheltering Sky*?

BOWLES: I wanted to put three characters together travelling through the desert. I didn't know what was going to happen and who these characters were. I knew that from a certain point the novel would write itself. It was like keeping a bird in a cage. At a certain point you have to open the cage and let the bird fly away, let him do what he wants. And this is the way I wrote *The Sheltering Sky*. Till the death of the hero I was, more or less, driving the story. From then on — once the cage door was open — I was driven by the story.

How would you describe your style?

BOWLES: I like using simple everyday words. My style is based on the contrast between deep emotional words and simple words. I hate showing off. The drama of an event comes from within it and not from the author's use of literary or rhetorical words.

Where did you write *The Sheltering Sky* ?

BOWLES: I wrote most of the story by travelling around the Sahara. I've been to all the places I described in the book, which I completed in the spring of 1948. I sent it to the publisher, but received a cold reply: *'The contract was for a novel. This is not a novel'*. I had to return the advance and look for another publisher.

Did you feel frustrated by the rejection?

BOWLES: I knew that sooner or later what I had written would be appreciated. I didn't get too upset about it. After all, it is not in my character to feel terribly hopeless or to be upset on account of a worrying situation. And in any case,

JANE BOWLES, 1963.
'Her death was a terrible ordeal as it was half of myself that I lost.'

I always had music. If I hadn't been successful as a writer, I would have continued to work as a musician. Music was like a blanket for me — it protected me.

Like the 'sheltering sky' in your novel...

BOWLES: We think of the sky as light and bright, but actually, if you could get beyond, you would find only space, infinite black space. And therefore I was saying, *'don't believe in the sky, don't believe in anything except the fact that it protects us from the dark, because beyond it is just blackness.'* That is the meaning of the title.

Critics have often talked about existentialism in connection with your work...

BOWLES: This does not seem to be at all accurate. According to the existentialists life is meaningless and man behaves gratuitously. But Sartre has a more optimistic vision than I have: he believes that it is possible, even necessary, for men to attain redemption, whereas I do not believe at all in the possibility of escaping from destiny. We can only curl up inside destiny like a cloud in the sky. I don't know whether I have been influenced by the fatalism of the Arabs and whether I have chosen to live amongst them because I see my fatalism mirrored in their fatalism.

You used to travel a lot...

BOWLES: If travelling today still meant taking ships, I would have gone on travelling. But taking the airplane for me isn't travelling. It's just going from one place to another in as little time as possible. When you go on a trip, you shouldn't know for how long. That's travelling. On my trips I used to take a lot of luggage with me. I remember once with Jane we had thirty suitcases and two big wardrobe trunks. And one trunk was stuffed only with Jane's shoes. Her mother had always told her that you needed a pair for every dress. So, that's

PAUL at the age of ten with his parents. *'My father couldn't bear to have my mother pay attention to this third person, me. Quite possibly my coming into existence was the result of an accident.'*

PAUL BOWLES (seated) with (from left) PETER ORLOWSKY, WILLIAM BURROUGHS, ALLEN GINSBERG, ALAN ANSEN, GREGORY CORSO, IAN SOMMERVILLE. *'I took Allen Ginsberg to Marakesh but this has not made me a poet of the beat generation.'*

why we had all this luggage. Of course, it is impossible to travel that way nowadays. Who would carry all those cases?

In your book you describe disintegration, lack of balance, the precariousness of individuals who are constantly in crisis — a crisis which involves the whole of Western culture...

BOWLES: The collapse of a culture which is already on the verge of breaking down is inevitable. When I arrived in Morocco in 1931 it was a very different world from today. Even the Sahara was different. The French were there and they were terribly racist. Once a haughty petty official said to me as he looked down at some Arabs, *'The day they learn to read and write, will be the day it's all over for us!'* And that's what has happened. The representatives of the so-called 'civilised' world are no longer here.

In other words, does this mean that the Western value system no longer works...?

BOWLES: The so-called Western 'values', what kind of values are they? I don't think, for instance, that the America of today is a country with values or 'culture': it is a huge monstrous 'non-culture', a 'non-civilisation'. It's a long time since I've been to America, but I have many friends who tell me what's going on there. It's an apocalypse.

Don't you miss the intellectual life of your country and of Europe?

BOWLES: I have always worked in intellectual solitude. For me, other American writers didn't exist. I know it is terribly egotistic on my part, but I didn't want any concurrence. That doesn't mean I thought I was the best writer. I simply didn't want to think of the existence of other writers. I would have asked myself too many questions. I wanted to be far away when the criticisms would appear. Yes, I read criticisms, but I am not there where they are published. It's a rather comfortable feeling being so far away...

PAUL BOWLES, Rembrandt Hotel, Tangier, 1951. *'When you go on a trip, you shouldn't know for how long. That's travelling.'*

TENNESSEE WILLIAMS and PAUL BOWLES, Tangier, 1951. *'At Tennessee's suggestion, I went to Rome to work with Luchino Visconti on a film called* Senso.'

PAUL BOWLES, 1983. *'I discovered that I couldn't express with music the negative side of myself which instead I was able to "paint" with words.'*

A PAGE FROM ONE OF PAUL BOWLES' NOTEBOOKS. *'One must accept one's own limitations as one accepts life and death, pain and pleasure. Only then can these natural defects be utilized to their fullest extent. Resistance cripples.'*

You once were called *'the guru of the Beat generation'* ...

BOWLES: In the sixties, at the time of the hippies, many came to Tangier to visit Jane and me. But they came here to see us as an object of curiosity. It was very unpleasant, not funny at all... Corso, Ginsberg and Orlowsky, they came together to Morocco and were with William Burroughs all the time. I knew them all personally, but I never belonged to their group. I took Allen Ginsberg to Marrakesh; but this has not made me a poet of the Beat generation.

What effect does it have on you, given your 'objectivity' as the author, to take part in the film and to play yourself?

BOWLES: Well, I felt I couldn't be there. In other words I hadn't invited myself when I wrote it. I would say, *'So, who is this person watching...?'* And Bertolucci would say, *'That's you watching your past life.'* He thinks *The Sheltering Sky* is autobiographical and there is no use telling him again that it isn't, because he believes that it is. And he told the actors that it was really about my life, that Kit was really Jane. And there is no way of denying that successfully — so I didn't try.

But there must be some autobiographical elements in *The Sheltering Sky*?

BOWLES: There are undoubtedly a whole series of situations or characters drawn from real life or linked to my personal experience. For example, the description of the death of Port is closely connected with a drug, *majoun*, which I had never tried before. I felt really ill when I took it and spent a horrible day suspended midway between life and death. And I experienced all the agonizing sensations which I describe: that feeling of the painful annihilation of the body. But all this helped me to evoke a scene, to write more convincingly about the situation which I wanted to describe — not ostentatiously displaying the details of an event. I used emotions, observations and impressions to create my characters and to give substance to a story which I had invented. The whole is blended together in the fabric of the novel and ends up by having its own existence. My personal life doesn't enter into it.

Are you suggesting that the role of the writer is only that of letting the characters and the story emerge from 'the indistinct magma' of his experiences and memories?

BOWLES: I think that it's good for the author to disappear behind his work, and not to show himself or steal his characters' roles. I try to achieve a certain impassivity in my portrayal.

In spite of everything, it seems that something of your personal convictions and sympathies emerge in your book. For example, you demonstrate a certain sympathy for Kit...

BOWLES: Yes, it's true.

Is this because Kit is on your side in the 'rebellion' against the established order?

BOWLES: Critics have always given arbitrary interpretations of my writing and I am accustomed to the fact that everyone attributes what he wishes to see in what I have written. It's true that I have a special affinity with Kit. But don't forget that at the end she disappears into thin air...

And what happens to her?

BOWLES: All these years I have also asked myself this question. It's a mystery. But thanks to Bertolucci's film and the public's reaction I may find some clues as to what happened to Kit.

PAUL BOWLES, 1955.
'I had not a specific single idea in my head with regard to writing fiction, neverthless I yearned for the experience of losing myself in a fictional world at the moment of creating it.'

FABIO TRONCARELLI, journalist and professor of Paleography at the University of Florence, writes for some of the leading Italian magazines. He has published several books, including the collection of poems *Discrezione* (1985) and the novel *Stella Polare* (1988).

The Marriage Melody

BY MILLICENT DILLON

When Paul Bowles met Jane Auer in 1937 in New York, he was twenty-six, a published poet and an established composer, blond, handsome, witty and charming, with a certain detachment in that charm. She was twenty-one, a writer as yet unpublished, small and dark with a mop of hennaed hair, elfin, fey, witty, endowed with a curious power that dazzled some and alienated others. He was capable of withholding himself from others, in self-protection and to protect his art. She knew little about self-defence, living almost continuously on the edge of anxiety. He drew a definite border between life and art. She could make no such separation.

▶ At their first meeting, they went with friends to an apartment in Harlem where they sat on the floor and smoked joints at fifty cents a piece. She did not speak to him though he tried to speak to her. Many years later she wrote two sentences about the meeting. *'He wrote music and was mysterious and sinister. The first time I saw him I said to a friend: He's my enemy.'*

▶ Two years later, they were married. On their honeymoon in Central America, he was drawn to the exotic and the strange, to mysterious places, as far from civilization as possible. She was fearful of crossing any borders, dreaded mountains, deserts, and unfamiliar landscapes, yet she tried to follow where he led. From Central America they travelled to Paris where, surrounded by a familiar civilized world, the strain on the marriage increased.

▶ Theirs was a marriage to which the word 'conventional' could hardly apply. Still, at the beginning, it aimed toward aspects of the conventional, sexually and in other ways. He supported her financially, she learned to cook, they shared a sexual relationship. But after their return to the US, the marriage changed and they lived separate sexual lives.

▶ It was to continue, however, as an intense and intimate and devoted relationship, lasting through journeys taken together and apart, through casual and not so casual affairs with others. In the early forties they went to Mexico, where Jane began a long affair with an older woman, Helvetia Perkins. In 1948, Jane followed Paul to Morocco, where she entered upon another long affair, this time with an illiterate Moroccan woman, Cherifa, a believer in magic potions.

▶ They were linked, even bound to each other in marriage through the intricacies of their creative lives. His image entered into her novel *Two Serious Ladies*, as the model for Mr Copperfield, the husband of Freda Copperfield, the 'serious' lady who seeks salvation through pleasure. (The other serious lady, Christina Goering, haunted by questions of sin, looks for redemption through the menacing power of men). Mr Copperfield emerges as the one 'sane' voice of the novel: he warns his wife simply not to repeat her past sufferings. He urges her to travel further with him into the jungle in Central America. She chooses, however, to stay behind in Panama City with the prostitute Pacifica to find the salvation she has always desired, a form of *'going to pieces'* by choice. Mr Copperfield goes on his way, an onlooker, intent upon his own journey out in the world, while the two serious ladies make their chosen journeys, *'piling sin upon sin'*. In her imagination Jane was willing to subject her own image (in the guise of the two serious ladies) to danger and to shattering, but she could not, or would not, do the same to the image of Paul. Unable to establish a clear boundary between her imaginative work and the life she lived, she protected his image in the novel.

▶ When Paul, however, drew upon Jane's image in life for the character of Kit Moresby in *The Sheltering Sky*, his imagination operated with no such restrictions. It is true that, at the beginning of the novel, Kit Moresby is the observer, while her husband Port is the protagonist. Port thinks of Kit back at the hotel, filing her nails and looking out over the town, while he sets out on his

JANE at the age of twenty-four. She was fearful of crossing any borders, dreaded mountains, deserts, and unfamiliar landscapes.

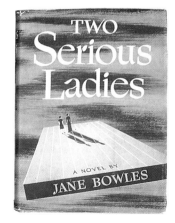

TWO SERIOUS LADIES, 1943, is the story of two women *'going to pieces'* as they persue their own eccentric paths to freedom.

For Jane fiction was also prophecy, so when she came to read 'The Sheltering Sky', she was terribly disturbed by the ending.

JANE with TRUMAN CAPOTE, TANGIER, 1949.

own mysterious sexual adventure in the Arab town. Port feels that '*the validity of his existence at that moment was predicated on the assumption that she had not moved, but was still sitting there.*' But by the end of the novel, Kit is no longer the spectator outside the action. After Port's death, she goes deeper and deeper into the Sahara and descends into darkness and madness.

❱ For the character of Kit, Paul initially called upon certain qualities that Jane had in life: her tendency to see things and events as omens, her fear that she could never imagine the worst that was in store for her, her susceptibility to feelings of guilt, her sudden, unpredictable changes of mood, her wit and her capacity for play. He has Kit trying to be 'agreeable', trying to be a 'dutiful wife', as Jane herself tried to be when she followed Paul to Morocco. He has Kit acknowledge her intense dependence on Port, just as Jane wrote to Paul of her own dependence upon him in her letters.

❱ But as the novel progresses, Kit changes. She who has felt guilt over her affair with Tunner, rejects it now. She who has wanted closeness with Port looks for detachment. With Port's death, in fact, she takes on his characteristics and ends up suffering, as terribly, if not more terribly, than he does.

❱ For Jane, fiction was also prophecy, so when she came to read *The Sheltering Sky*, she was terribly disturbed by the ending. In later years she would tell Paul that she feared that he had predicted her ending in Kit's ending. He, in turn, would become very upset, telling her Kit's fate was fiction, an act of the imagination, not prophecy. As it happened, Jane suffered a debilitating stroke in 1958 at the age of forty-one, and was never really well again. She died in 1973 in a convent hospital in Malaga, after a descent into darkness that some called the loss of reason. At the end, she was unable to see, unable to talk and unable to move. Yet Paul, going to visit her and sitting by her bedside, held on to the belief that she was aware of all that was happening, that she had not truly descended into darkness.

❱ In a fragment in a notebook Jane once wrote of a husband and wife, having just come to North Africa, sitting at an iron table in a café, talking of the journey he wanted to take into the desert, a journey she didn't want to make. She used the words '*their marriage melody*' to describe what went on between them. The '*marriage melody*' between Paul and Jane was, of course, a sound that no outsider could ever hear. Yet this much can be said: in *The Sheltering Sky* Paul has Port say to Kit, just as he is about to die, that he has never realized until then that he has lived his life 'through' her. It was a statement Paul was to repeat in the years after Jane's death about his own life with Jane, that he had lived 'through' her. And she, in a letter to him in 1948, writing of her pursuit of the Moroccan woman, says, '*I wonder too if I would bother with all of this if you didn't exist... It is the way I feel about my writing too. Would I bother if you didn't exist?*'

MILLICENT DILLON has published three works of fiction, she is the author of the play *She is in Tangier,* based on the life of Jane Bowles. She is the author of the authorized biography on Jane Bowles *A Little Original Sin. The Life and Work of Jane Bowles,* and has edited *Out in the World: Selected Letters of Jane Bowles, 1935-1970.* She has also written *After Egypt. Isadora Duncan and Mary Cassatt* (Dutton-Nal, New York, 1990).

JANE and the photographer CECIL BEATON at one of the many parties held in Tangier in 1948.

The Physiology of Feelings

AN INTERVIEW BY RENATO LEYS

BERTOLUCCI: While I was in the final stages of editing *The Last Emperor*, and just as I was finishing with China, the inevitable question popped up again : 'What should I do next?' After the film on Pu Yi, in which the man's private history became intertwined with HISTORY in capital letters, I was on the lookout for a subject that would allow me to put the soul under a microscope.

How did you get to know Bowles' novel?

BERTOLUCCI: For a number of years, I had been hearing about *The Sheltering Sky* from at least three friends: Mark Peploe, Ferdinando Scarfiotti and Marilyn Goldin. They were members of a secret society, the sect of Paul Bowles' 'worshippers'. I had been holding out, resisting their pressure and their best efforts to ensnare me, perhaps because I was irritated by the fanaticism with which they spoke of the book.

❭ Overcoming my natural suspicion, I finally read the book on one of my trips to China. At once I tought: 'This is a movie!'. I was fascinated by the idea of these 'figures in a landscape', so like the paintings of Caspar David Friedrich. At the same time, I had the feeling that the story of Port and Kit would give me the possibility of exploring the *anatomy* of the characters even more than their *psychology*. I suppose that my secret ambition was to shoot a kind of endoscopic film, using a fibre-optic lens!

Your first impression of the book?

BERTOLUCCI: Suffering. At a certain point in the story, Port walks out onto a sloping plain from which you sense that there is simply no return. Only then do we realize that this 'odour of death' began on the first page of the novel. I identified so strongly with Port during his agony that I suffered physical pains I had never felt before. It was an overwhelming emotion that I couldn't explain. Confronting that emotion by making the film was the only way of exorcising it.

❭ So, three years later, as the Chinese chapter came to a close, I felt a strange kind of nostalgia for those pains. Before making any decisions, however, I travelled to Tangier with my co-writer Mark Peploe in order to meet the elusive writer Paul Bowles. He had not replied to the telegram sent to his legendary PO Box. We met at his flat, located in a shoddily built fifties apartment-block. The first impression was that of an extraordinarily elegant man, but consciously outmoded in his dress. He seemed physically fragile, but somehow also a man of iron. Invulnerable. Once his cover was blown, Paul seemed to me to be revealed as intimately delinquent, almost without restraints. That's his particular fascination. In the depths of the liquid blue gaze of this cautious eighty-year-old man lurks one of the wildest natures you could imagine.

❭ A few hours later, in front of the entrance of the Hotel El Minzah, I was the victim of an assault that might have ended very badly. Faced with death flashing in the eyes of a Moroccan boy wielding a knife, my wallet taken, and gripped by an overwhelming anxiety 'à la Genet', at that moment any remaining doubts vanished. I had to make *The Sheltering Sky*.

A lot has been said about the fact that the protagonists of the film are based directly on Paul and Jane Bowles.

BERTOLUCCI: *The Sheltering Sky* is a profoundly literary novel, giving a lot of room for its characters' thoughts. By its very nature, cinema has to leave at lot of room for what happens. There are some beautiful literary films like Wenders'

CHALK CLIFF ON RÜGEN, 1818, by C.D. FRIEDRICH. *'While reading* The Sheltering Sky *I was fascinated by the idea of these "figures in a landscape" so like the paintings of Caspar David Friedrich.'*

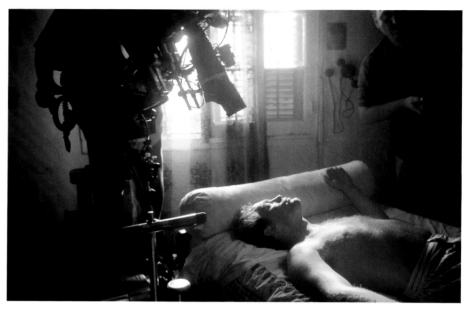

JOHN MALKOVICH under the 'microscope'. *'I was on the lockout for a subject that would allow me to put the soul under a microscope.'*

Wings of Desire, but I was headed in another direction. One of our concerns while writing the screenplay was that of filtering the literary values of the book. The goal was to arrive at some sort of 'physiology of feelings', substituting the inner voices with the physical presence of Kit and Port. From the start, we wondered how much of Paul and Jane's story had found its way into the book. Then I had the idea of building our characters by 'drawing from life' — from the original models.

But Bowles has always denied that the book is autobiographical...

BERTOLUCCI: Certainly, half of this writer's life has been spent defending his privacy — though recently he has begun to admit a few things. Paul now maintains that in creating Kit he was inspired by Jane in the same way a painter is inspired by a model. He liked the example I gave — that of Caravaggio witnessing the recovery of the body of a woman drowned in the Tiber and then remembering that livid corpse and painting *The Death of the Virgin*. Once you have got over the false problem of the 'autobiographical' nature of the work, I think the most important point is that the mystery and secret of Port and Kit revealed in the film, is not far removed from the mystery and secret of Paul and Jane.

Beyond the character of Port, Bowles is also physically present on the screen...

BERTOLUCCI: A few days before the shooting started, I suddenly had this feeling that something was missing. The 'literature' was totally absent. Together with Mark, I decided to insert Paul into the film. Through the physical presence of the novel's writer, we would represent the literature itself. I don't think there are many examples of this, where the author of a book plays himself on the screen. But how do you direct Paul Bowles? I just told him one thing: I would like to see on your face the sorrow of memory, the pain of remembering.

And the actors? How do they match up to the characters in the book and in the screenplay?

BERTOLUCCI: I think it was one of the most difficult and tiring casting jobs I've faced. In my mind, I imagined Port and Kit as the elegant children of Scott and Zelda Fitzgerald — beautiful and damned. I needed two American actors

BERTOLUCCI directing DEBRA WINGER, who plays Kit. *'Debra has to identify completely with her character. From day one of the shooting there is no difference for her between the film and life itself.'*

DEBRA WINGER and JOHN MALKOVICH. *'I needed two American actors whose chief attraction was the intelligence that shows on their faces.'*

SCOTT and ZELDA FITZGERALD in 1920 on their honeymoon. *'I imagined Port and Kit as the elegant children of Scott and Zelda Fitzgerald — beautiful and damned.'*

JILL BENNETT and TIMOTHY SPALL who play the Lyles. *'I was looking for two actors a bit sinister, a bit comic, almost caricatures of themselves, but always suggesting in some way that they are bearers of death.'*

JOHN MALKOVICH plays Port. *'John would slouch onto the set, and then as soon as the cameras rolled he'd have all the lightness of a ballet dancer.'*

CAMPBELL SCOTT, who plays Tunner, with BERNARDO BERTOLUCCI. *'Of the three protagonists, he is the one who came closest to expressing the 'body language' so typical of the forties.'*

ERIC VU-AN who plays Belqassim, and DEBRA WINGER. *'The rapport between Belqassim and Kit is delicate, almost something like between a little boy and a woman.'*

whose chief attraction was the intelligence that shows on their faces. Thus I came to choose Debra Winger and John Malkovich, so different in their approach to their role, and yet so harmonious in creating a couple that is both symbiotic and unhappy.

▶ Debra has to identify completely with her character. From day one of the shooting, there is no difference for her between the film and life itself. She turns her life upside down to enrich the film just as she might turn the film upside down to enrich her life. I've never seen an actor suffer so much or be so obsessively and unceasingly in contact with her character. This way of working, which creates a constant emotional tension, is not unfamiliar to me. I, too, when I'm shooting, often fail to distinguish between my life and the film that I'm making.

▶ On the other hand, John Malkovich walks into the shot aided only by his own intuition. He succeeds in becoming the character by nimbly leaping over the whole process of rationalization. Or at least it seems that way. But who knows what goes on in John's head the night before he's acting? He's really something out of mythology. To me John appears like a centaur — these strong soccer-player thighs — whereas the upper part of his body seems softer, becoming at times almost effeminate. (In the same manner, Debra's incredibile energy at times seems to have something almost boyish about it). John would slouch onto the set, and then as soon as the cameras rolled, he'd have all the lightness of a ballet dancer. In any case, right now I cannot imagine any other Kit and Port than Debra Winger and John Malkovich.

But for the part of Tunner you chose someone completely unknown...

BERTOLUCCI: Campbell Scott fills me with pride. He's very young, almost a beginner in films, with a background in theatre. I believed in him and was rewarded with a consummate performance. He demonstrated all the experience of a seasoned actor. Of the three of them he's the one who came closest to expressing the 'body language' so typical of the forties. I'm pleased to think that I discovered him.

❱ On the other hand, Jill Bennett and Timothy Spall — who no doubt some people in England will think of as vaguely 'hammy' — represent the great tradition of English theatre. To be honest, what I was looking for were two actors who recall the minor characters of John Huston — types like Peter Lorre, Elisha Cook Jr or Sidnyey Greenstreet or Robert Morley. You know, a bit sinister, a bit comic, almost caricatures of themselves, but always suggesting in some way that they are bearers of death.

If John Malkovich is a false ballet dancer, Eric Vu-An, who plays Belqassim, is the real thing...

BERTOLUCCI: Yes, Eric is one of the most extraordinary dancers of the 'post *Nouvelle Vague'* in international ballet. I have asked myself how I came to make such an eccentric choice. Perhaps the explanation is that Belqassim is a figure who, both in the book and in the film, stands outside all known psychological convention. Hiding beneath that turban is desire, the desirer and the desired — all at once. He is the man without a face and without a country. The true nomad. I also discovered that the Tuaregs are great narcissists; the sand is the mirror in which their shadows are reflected.

The Sheltering Sky seems as much a road movie as a love story: an escape that leads them to the middle of nowhere...

BERTOLUCCI: The children of Scott and Zelda have discovered that all the glamour that fired the stories of Fitzgerald is gone, cancelled for ever by the war. So Paul and Kit, Jane and Port, turn their back on the United States — on New York and Long Island and the mentality that's associated with all the values of the 'American dream' — to head off to another continent, in search of something different. And this is how they wind up in North Africa, in exactly the same place where existentialism was even at that moment being born.

❱ Port and Kit love each other, but they know that they are not going to succeed ever again in being happy together. To love without being happy. Love as a mutual blackmail that unites two people, each of whom is aware of the absence of happiness. Two persons who love one another, adore each other, but are unhappy. They fail to experience love for its own sake, but rather as something horribly conflictive and endlessly sad, and their journey across the desert is an effort to patch up a relationship that's shattered into a thousand pieces. It is paralleled by the 'journey' they are making into themselves in search of their own identity — for they have lost a sense of identity in the conjugal osmosis, in the ceaseless inter-mirroring of their personalities one against the other. If I look around me today, I see lots of people in this same state.

❱ After we shot the scene in which Port and Kit try to make love among the rocks on top of the ridge, I was speaking on the phone with my wife, Clare, and I told her how painful a day it had been for me and for the actors. It's very sad speaking about a couple divided, as it were, by an invisible wall. The next day, Clare sent me a fax in which she wrote: *'While you were filming about a couple divided by an invisible wall, the Berlin Wall came down'*. It was a shock for me, because I was completely unaware of what was happening in Europe. The selfishness of unhappiness. By becoming so absorbed in the pain of this unhappy couple of 1947, I'd lost touch with the outside world. The news brought me back.

Bowles' book is universal, yet strangely topical...

BERTOLUCCI: The book, which was a success when it came out, soon became the bible of this 'secret society' I was talking about. Then, in the past two or three years it has burst again onto the literary scene. In effect, I think the novel was ahead of its time, since the isolated melancholy experienced by Port and Kit forty years ago has now assumed epidemic proportions. All that we said

BERNARDO BERTOLUCCI in Niger. *'One January afternoon in Agadez market, I discovered that reality, when it is desired, courted, provoked, within a few seconds is able to transform itself into pure fiction.'*

about the paradox of love condemned to continue even in the absence of happiness is a notion very typical of the late eighties. We could also speak of the renewed search for alternative values developing as a reaction to the overdose of consumerism, and it isn't surprising that existentialism should once again take hold of the popular imagination. Due to the media bombardment, the encroaching desert, so pervasive in the book, also pervades our thoughts now. A desert world about to become tomorrow's reality. A symptom of the greenhouse effect.

So as you were saying, love equals unhappines. But whenever separation takes place, it's always a terrible thing...

BERTOLUCCI with the director of the 2nd unit, FERNAND MOSZKOWICZ.

BERTOLUCCI: One day, just before Christmas, Port Moresby slipped from the final stage of agony into death. I remember feeling sick as a dog. More precisely, I was totally identifying with John Malkovich's suffering, and I couldn't bear the separation from Port. Or was it that I feared being abandoned by John? This is a perfect example of how, all too often, I end up by confusing real life with fiction. Naturally, after all that anxiety, came a feeling of liberation. John Malkovich left, and, miraculously, I succeeded in forgetting both him and Port. The very next day we began the last part of the film, with Kits its only protagonist. I shot it all in a state of trance. It is the 'chapter' in which psychology is replaced by something else. The part where the inhuman effort of taking up the tale every day, carrying it forward again and again, is replaced by something new and unexpected. All of a sudden there is the sensation of relief as if you are being drawn along by the adventure of the film, and that by now it is travelling on its own legs — slender but indefatigable, like those of a camel.

It is also the moment in which the film starts to betray the book...

BERTOLUCCI: Yes, my great 'betrayal' took place just before filming the first night that Kit and Belqassim spend together in the desert. I was standing there next to the dunes, under the moon, looking at the camels and the Tuaregs in the camp site, listening to the flutes, and all of a sudden, I had this feeling of falsehood. At any rate, there was this strong sensation that the last part of the film risked being crushed beneath the weight of cliché. Then, discussing with the Tuaregs I learnt they deny that rape, or any form of carnal violence, exists in their culture. Theirs is a matriarchal society. So it occurred to me perhaps the end of the book was a kind of fantasy on Bowles' part. It was not to be taken too seriously.

▶ If suddenly changing the screenplay means taking a risk, then it also means the ecstasy of improvisation. In any case, there was nothing else to be done. This is why there is no explicit violence in the film. In this sense the film is different from the book. The rapport between Belqassim and Kit is delicate, almost like something between a little boy and a woman. What I was trying to capture in the young man Belqassim was the same slightly 'obscene' innocence we see in the child who spies on them as they make love in the mud room.

The moment the caravan arrives, you feel like you are watching another film...

BERTOLUCCI: Only later did I realize that the narrative change implied an important change of style as well. Once in Niger, immersed in the vast African crowd, I began to 'record' this reality — and Debra hurled into the midst of it — with the 'natural' documentary eye of a Rossellini or a Jean Rouch. And so I discovered, in that January afternoon, in Agadez market, that the reality, when it is desired, courted, provoked, in a few seconds is able to transform itself into pure fiction.

And somtimes into dreams as well... But as described by Bowles, Kit's long delerium is usually associated more with 'madness' than 'dreaming'.

BERTOLUCCI: In the novel, Kit is the victim of a painful loss of identity. Immediately following Port's death, there is a strange fusion of the two of them. Kit 'metabolizes' or absorbs all that Port was and she brings his dream to its extreme consequence. By yielding the temptation of losing herself in exotic adventures, she imitates him. She prolongs Port's obsession to annihilate himself in risk. Thus Port continues to live on in Kit, just as on the screen Jane Bowles continues to live in Debra. So that at the end everyone involved seems to flow together into the gaze of Bowles. They have understood that in those eyes is their only salvation: nothingness, the absolute night.

RENATO LEYS is a painter, a poet and a close friend to Bernardo Bertolucci. He has travelled extensively in the Orient and North Africa. He is the author of an unpublished biography of Victor Segalen.

'All at once there is a sensation of relief as if you are being drawn along by the adventure of the film, and by now it is travelling on its own legs — slender but indefatigable, like those of a camel.'

'I discovered that the Tuaregs are great narcisists; the sand is the mirror in which their shadows are reflected.'

BERNARDO BERTOLUCCI: *'I identified so strongly with Port during his agony that I suffered physical pain I had never felt before.'*

The Road from Parma

BY GEORGES-LOUIS BOURGEOIS

In 1962, the 'ragazzi' from THE GRIM REAPER, inspired by a Pasolini story about the murder of a prostitute, were only slightly younger than their director.

A young bourgeois of Parma revolts against the established order by having an affair with his own aunt in BEFORE THE REVOLUTION, 1964.

▶ Los Angeles, April 1988. In the space of a single evening *The Last Emperor* became part of the Hollywood legend, collecting no less than nine Academy Awards, including the Oscar for 'Best Film'. It was a glorious moment for the poet turned film-maker whose work had too often been passed over by the juries of the major film festivals.

▶ Cut to North Italy, March 1941. Bernardo Bertolucci was born just outside Parma, a few miles from the estate of the opera composer Giuseppe Verdi. His mother, who is of Australian-Irish descent, taught literature, history and geography, whilst his father, the well-known writer Attilio Bertolucci, combined teaching art history with a career as a poet and film critic for the local newspaper *Gazzetta di Parma*.

▶ As a child, Bernardo divided his spare time '*between cows and books*'. As soon as he was old enough, he began to accompany his father on the long tram ride into town where together the two enjoyed the wonders of the cinema. Small surprise then to find the fifteen-year-old adolescent spending his holidays making two short films on a borrowed 16mm camera, funding them out of his pocket-money. The first film was about three children who get lost in a forest one midsummer afternoon; the second filmed the traditional autumn slaughter of a pig in his parents' farmyard.

▶ Meanwhile, the Bertolucci family had moved to Rome were they lived in the same building as Pier Paolo Pasolini. Already an established writer, who was indebted to Attilio Bertolucci for the publication of his first novel, *Ragazzi di Vita*, Pasolini was about to work on his début film. In turn, he was to help foster the career of his patron's son and invited him to work, as a first assistant, on *Accattone*. The year was 1961. Luck was on Bernardo's side, since in the flurry of *Accattone*'s success a producer 'seized with a flash of madness' immediately asked the aspiring director to write and then direct *The Grim Reaper*, based on another Pasolini tale of prostitution and poverty in Rome. At twenty-one, Bertolucci became the youngest professional director in the history of cinema.

▶ Though well received abroad, the film was hammered by the Italian press, when cast into the arena of the 1962 Venice Film Festival. The fact that this wunderkind had just scooped up the prestigious Viareggio '*Opera Prima*' literary prize for his first collection of poems, *In Search of Mystery*, didn't help. Some even suggested that 'Bertolucci Junior' should give up cinema and

BERNARDO BERTOLUCCI: *'I suppose that my secret ambition was to shoot a kind of endoscopic film, using a fibre-optic lens!'*

BERTOLUCCI on location with co-writer MARK PEPLOE.

BERTOLUCCI discussing a shot with his cinematographer VITTORIO STORARO.

In 1966, Bernardo Bertolucci (on the right) shot together with Julian Beck (on the left) and the Living Theatre the *AGONY* episode in the film *LOVE AND ANGER,* released in 1969.

Giulio Brogi plays the dual role of a resistance fighter assassinated by the fascists and his son enquiring into his death thirty years later in *THE SPIDER'S STRATAGEM,* 1969.

What happens when an introverted intellectual from Dostoyevsky meets his perfect double - an anarchist of May '68? (Pierre Clémenti in *PARTNER,* 1968)

concentrate on his verse. *'Poetry was my father's kingdom, not mine. So I had to invent my own language. And my language was to tell stories in films.'*

▶ Bertolucci's second feature, *Before the Revolution*, written with his friend Gianni Amico and made in 1964, was a more directly personal film. It told the story of a young Marxist from the Parma bourgeoisie and his gradual disenchantment with the consumeristic aspirations of the working class in which he had placed all his hopes. The film, however, did not find its audience until early 1968. That angry young generation felt they were hearing a prophetic echo of their own dissatisfaction, whilst French, English and American critics joined together to praise 'the new Orson Welles from Parma'. He was still ignored in Italy.

▶ The late release of *Before the Revolution* confined the director to a long period of inactivity, barely compensated by a few documentaries and the '*Agony*' episode of *Love and Anger*, which initiated him into the experimental methods of Julian Beck's Living Theatre. But Bertolucci's fortune was to change in 1967, when Sergio Leone asked him to write the storyline for his new spaghetti western, *Once Upon a Time in the West*.

▶ Back in the saddle, he persuaded his cousin Giovanni Bertolucci to embark on film production. By April 1968, they were ready to start shooting *Partner*, a contemporary variation of Dostoyevsky's *The Double*. The film, overtaken by reality, was rewritten daily, adapting to the events of May in Paris and becoming a chronicle of the encounter between an introverted intellectual and his perfect twin, an anarchist who took the creed of '*all power to the imagination!*' to its very extreme.

▶ In 1969, in direct contrast to the frenetic neurosis of *Partner*, an Olympian serenity descended on *The Spider's Stratagem*, which was conceived in the first weeks of Bernardo's psychoanalysis. This was a free adaptation from Borges' *Theme of the Traitor and the Hero*. Contained within the dreamlike maze of a small town which could have come straight out of a surrealistic western set in the Po valley around Parma, this journey through the deepest regions of the human psyche follows step by step a son's investigation into the mysterious murder of his father, a martyr of the Italian resistance, thirty years before. The truth is that the father had been shot by his companions for revealing a futile — and possibly counter-productive — plot against Mussolini. But nobody will ever know how far the 'informer' had foreseen that through his action and subsequent proposal to disguise his own execution as a fascist assassination, he would revive the cause of the armed struggle all over the country.

▶ The editing of *The Spider's Stratagem* was postponed as Bertolucci went immediately into pre-production of *The Conformist*, in the summer of 1969.

Based on the novel by the director's friend Alberto Moravia, the film once again plays out the Oedipal myth against the background of Mussolini's Italy and captures the fascist age perfectly. It was to be Bertolucci's first commercial success and in spite of the experimental interests, the film nevertheless turned out to be very appealing to a wide audience and refreshingly original. Francis Coppola heralded it as the first 'classic' of the new era of cinema.

◗ Bertolucci could now be assured of his standing as a film-maker. Critical evaluation of his next film *Last Tango in Paris*, however, was eclipsed by its 'succès de scandal'. '*A film that altered the face of an art form*' said *The New Yorker*'s Pauline Kael, rightly comparing the event to the opening of Stravinsky's *Rite of Spring*, in terms of its innovation and the reaction to it. Indeed, the spectacle of one of Hollywood's ageing icons having his soul stripped bare has provided cinema history with one of its more significant moments. It is hard to know, though, to what extent the crowd flocking to the movie theatre hoping for a sex romp actually perceived the immense emotional candour of this twisted dance of love and death. Whatever their response, the movie became a box office smash and gave Bertolucci a new financial credibility, even if its success rested on a huge misunderstanding.

◗ The film-maker could now command the kind of budget which would enable him to make the monumental *1900*. Written in collaboration with his brother Giuseppe Bertolucci and his editor Kim Arcalli, this five-hour-long epic, tells the parallel stories of landowner and peasant who are both born on the same day at the same farm near Parma. The history of twentieth-century Italy is traced through these class enemies raised as blood brothers, in whom we can discern the two faces of an *author* perpetually haunted by the inescapable guilt of not being born poor. Certainly *1900* is a heroic film worthy of Erich von Stroheim, and it was to receive the same fate in the U.S. market place as the grand film-maker's most ambitious projects. Cut from 320 to 240 minutes, *1900* closed after only a few days.

In THE CONFORMIST (1971) Dominique Sanda and Stefania Sandrelli embody two opposite destinies. A dramatic choice for Trintignant.

For the first time in history, an 'Hollywood icon' agreed to unmask before the camera (Maria Schneider and Marlon Brando in LAST TANGO IN PARIS, 1973).

The film *1900* portrays the long fight against Fascism in the Parma countryside, as seen through the friendship of a landowner and a peasant (Robert de Niro and Gerard Depardieu, 1976)

▶ It was not until 1979 that Bertolucci released *La Luna*. The film is the story of an American opera singer, on tour in Italy, and her relationship with her drug addict son. The theme of incest, alluded to in several of his other films as a metaphor for social transgression, is here fully explored. The stylistic key to *La Luna* was the manner in which operatic conventions started taking over the singer's personal life. Bertolucci also attempted to offset the melodrama with 'sophisticated comedy'. The result proved to be a bit too unusual for some.

▶ Two years later, the director's usual audience was to be equally bemused by *The Tragedy of a Ridiculous Man*. Set again in the familiar Parma countryside, but this time one that is modern and industrialised, its protagonists are the new farming rich. Their wealth now makes them targets for kidnapping and ransom demands. Film noir goes rural, and it was, perhaps, some kind of compensation for Bertolucci's frustration at never seeing his long-cherished project of Dashiell Hammett's *Red Harvest* come to a successful fruition.

▶ A chance reading of the autobiography of Pu Yi, the last Emperor of China, in 1982, gave the director the idea for his next film. It paralleled many of the strands threaded through his own work and enabled him the opportunity to knit them all together for the first time. The People's Court at the end of *1900* had failed to transform the landowner into a humble peasant; would Pu Yi's 're-education' succeed in turning the Lord of Ten Thousand Years into a humble citizen? In other words, how far is it possible for an individual to free himself from the burden of memory and history in order to be reborn? If it is true that each of Bernardo Bertolucci's films is one step further towards 'maturity', then *The Last Emperor* represented both the culmination of a long search and the starting point for a new departure.

▶ Back from this distant journey which, as always, was to prove to be primarily a journey of self-discovery, linked by the tiniest threads, the director of *The Spider's Stratagem* had an appointment for tea in the desert with Paul Bowles, author of *The Spider's House*. They were to journey together across the bare labyrinth of the Sahara — *'the only place in the world where even memory disappears'*.

GEORGES-LOUIS BOURGEOIS, Professor at the University of Buenos Aires, is the author of *The Italian Cinema: Myth and Reality* (Aleph, 1981). He is currently writing *The Universal History of Fiction*.

Anouk Aimé is the French wife of a rich ham and cheese exporter whose only child has been kidnapped in *THE TRAGEDY OF A RIDICULOUS MAN,* 1981.

An American opera singer on tour in Italy will break the last taboo to save her son from drug addiction (Jill Clayburgh and Laura Betti in *LA LUNA,* 1979).

Bernardo Bertolucci during the shooting of *THE LAST EMPEROR,* 1987.

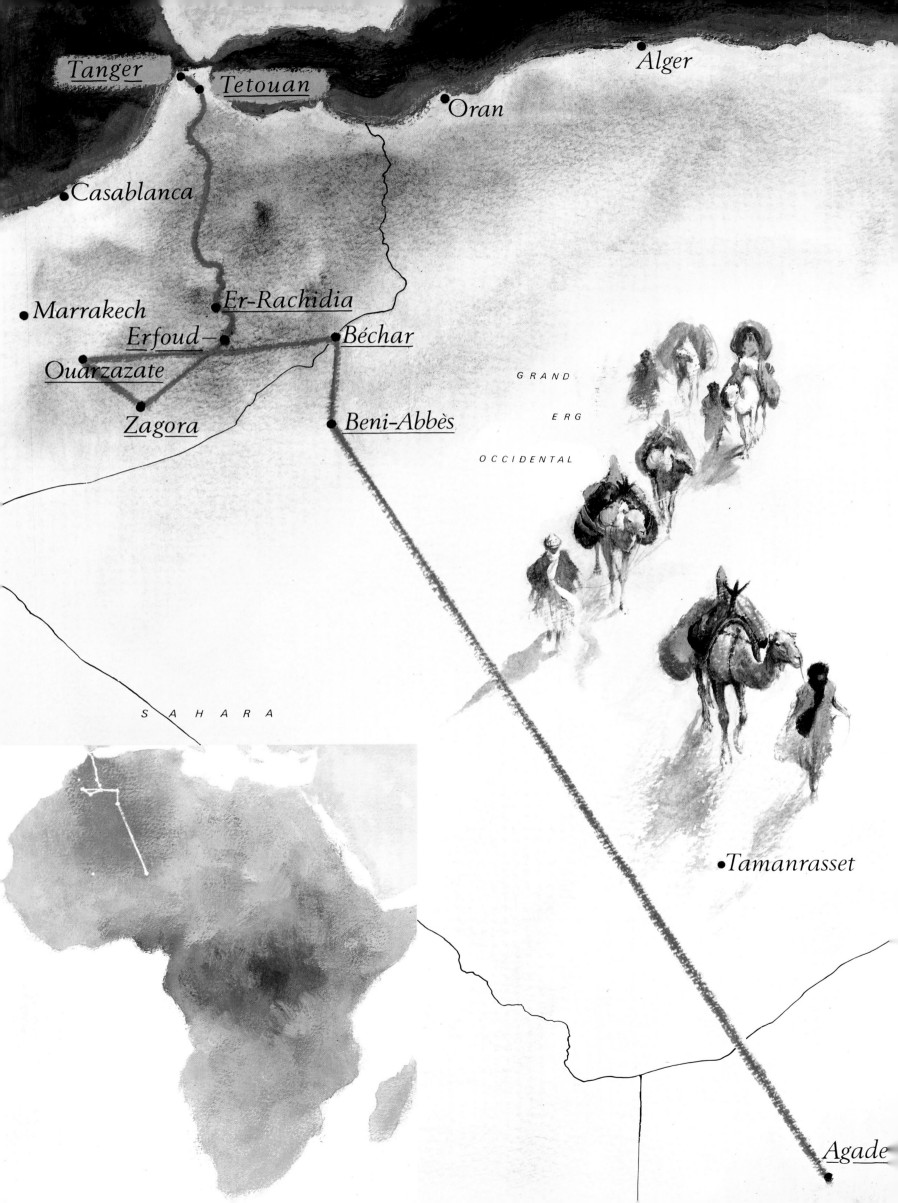

Tanger

Tetouan

Alger

Oran

Casablanca

Marrakech · Er-Rachidia

Erfoud—

Ouarzazate · Béchar

Zagora · Beni-Abbès

GRAND

ERG

OCCIDENTAL

SAHARA

Tamanrasset

Agade

Twelve Locations in Search of an Author

BY FABIEN S. GERARD

MOROCCO

TANGIER
From September 21st to October 27th, 1989

▶ The novel *The Sheltering Sky* actually starts with Kit, Port and Tunner disembarking in the Algerian harbour of Oran. However, a different choice was made in the film. Oran was substituted for the legendary free port of Tangier, where West meets East, and North meets South. After so many years of sailing the seas, this colourful gateway to Africa was where Paul Bowles finally dropped his anchor.

▶ The unexpected arrival of HRH King Hassan II's yacht from Gibraltar immediately put paid to our schedule so painstakingly worked out over the long hot summer. Because of this event, the Moroccan Security police barred the film crew for three days from the port. The filming resumed with a long intense close-up of an elderly boulevardier sitting in the shadows at the back of a French café. As through a looking-glass, before his very eyes, he watches the characters his imagination had created some forty years earlier become reality. A perfect homage to the author of the novel.

▶ On the morning of September 21st, under the 'oceanic' gaze of Paul Bowles, only a few minutes seemed necessary for the technicians to familiarize themselves with this opening set. It was alive to the exhuberant rythm of Charles Trenet's forties' hit *Je Chante* chosen as background music to the scene. The crew had worked on *The Last Emperor* and soon each of us had taken up our place within the 'family' as if scarcely a night had passed since we all had been working together in China.

▶ The old colonial boulevards, the Grand Hotels and the dream-like labyrinth of the Medina, were to be the backdrop of our daily lives until late October. These, too, were the settings for both the beginning and the ending of the film, since the exigencies of film budgeting necessitated that the epilogue of the film — Kit's return to Tangier from her long Saharan voyage — be shot when we were only in the fourth week of filming. So faithful to his customary practice, our director gave himself an option of shooting four different endings, as the final encounter between Bowles and Kit filmed in two separate locations — the French café with its Western decor and the heights of the old Arab town of Tetouan. In either location, when Paul Bowles asks his heroine whether she has lost her way, Kit's reply is '*Yes*' in one version and '*No*' in the other. Only the internal logic of the rest of the action will decide which will be the last scene of the film. This choice will be made at the latest possible moment during the editing.

ERFOUD
From October 28th to November 7th, 1989

▶ Flooding rains greeted our charter plane in Er-Rachidia after a one hour flight over the Atlas Mountains. Unprecedented, there had been no rains in the area for eight years. The crew, all one hundred and sixty of them, twenty trucks and a countless quantity of luggage were marooned. Two wadis had broken their banks and the roads to Erfoud were impassable for over two days. The producer was gnawing his fingers at the expenses of the delay, but Bernardo was trying to be philosophical: as an 'ex-farm boy', he jokingly suggested his presence had

brought the blessing of. rain to the drought-stricken region.

▶ As the waters retreated, the heat returned, and with it the flies. Ironically, though, there were not enough of them to complete a scene in a bus with our three protagonists on their way to Ain Krorfa. To create the effect of 'black snow' descending on the passengers, more than three millions laboratory-bred flies were imported from Italy. They arrived in hermetically sealed containers and awaited the appropriate moment to be freed by a neately-turbaned specialist, planted in the middle of the over-crowded bus.

▶ We then moved to the sordid patios of the small. town of Rissani where in the sorrounding of Ain Krokfa's Hotel Majestic — slightly more 'majestic' than its name suggests — John Malkovich was ro remark upon one of those improvised lines for which he has a special talent.

▶ However most of the time spent in this area would be devoted to the dramatic arrival of Port and Kit at the gates of El Ga'a, filmed in the dusty market of Gla Gla. There is where Port loses consciousness when he gets off the bus and suddenly collapses in front of Kit, before sinking into the delirium from which he was never to recover. The sequence owes much of its success to Brahim, the young black with the white turban who helps Kit find her way to the Hotel du Ksar. Picked out from the crowd of local extras that very morning, a few minute were sufficient to allow Brahim to complete the perfect understanding of his role.

▶ In the course of the next few days, the steadicam operator kept following the desperate race of Kit and her guide through the maze of dry mud passageways of Maadid. As Port was beginning his solitary agony, an irresistible attraction was forged between these two beings — Kit and her guide — whose worlds were so far apart, but who, without even realizing it, were now holding hands. Fascinated, Bernardo witnessed with growing excitement the way in which the shadow of Belqassim had subtly, and unexpectedly, cast itself into the very heart of the story.

TETOUAN. Paul Bowles, who plays himself in the film, awaits the call for '*action*' to meet Kit in one of the different endings imagined by his director.

Bertolucci draws his actors aside to discuss the love scene at the top of the ridge.

As the local peasants blessed the crew for having brought the rain, the actors were wrapped in the only pieces of blue sky visible around — sky-blue blanket.

For two days the steadicam operator followed Kit's desperate race to the Hotel du Ksar.

ZAGORA
November 10th and 11th, 1989

❱ It took a whole day's travel over a stony road to reach Zagora. Situated halfway between Erfoud and Ouarzazate, the place was to be the shortest stop of the entire filming. Within forty-eight hours, the end of the 'bicycle ride' sequence was completed, as well as the delicate love scene at the top of the ridge overlooking the Moroccan desert. A platform built above the precipice supported the two cameras focused upon thpainful embraces of Port and Kit among the rocks. The actors were protected from the harsh sun by a large canopy, which served to create, old day long, the subdued light of sunset. Port's line '*The sky is so strange here, almost solid...*' took a bizarre double meaning as John Malkovich's upturned face was only inches from the large white sheet. At the end of the day's shooting, this artificial 'sheltering sky' was removed to reveal that the sun was setting for real.

OUARZAZATE
From November 11th to December 1st, 1989

❱ Without even having time to memorize the room number of our third hotel in this fast-paced journey, the entire crew kept heading south. We set out at dawn. The sun was setting when Ouarzazate appeared in the distance. Nowadays, the old town walls have been engulfed under the tidal wave of foreign money brought in over the last two decades by large-scale productions such as *Lawrence of Arabia* and *The Man Who Would Be King*. The only area largely untouched is the Kasbah, a location which we had to share with a German TV crew for a whole week. They were shooting inside the Kasbah's main courtyard while we ventured in its innermost recesses. Duly shored up to support the weight of our presence, the corridors of the huge palace lead, in the film, to the rooms of the unpretentious *Hotel Transatlantique* in Bou Noura.
❱ First, however, our actors had to complete a former episode in a pretty disagreeable chronological disorder. The scenes that take place on the terrace of the hotel in Boussif were shot in an entirely reconstructed replica in the hamlet of Ait Saoun. The set perfectly matched the pyramidal glass roof crowning the Tangier patio where the interiors of the sequence had been shot in October.
❱ Port who has arrived by car with the Lyles, is now having breakfast on the terrace. He awaits Kit and Tunner, who chose to travel together by rail. Bowles' attentive readers will recall the description of the 'picturesque' sunrise which serves as backdrop to the first pages of Chapter XI. Faithfully recreated in the screenplay, this detail was to receive poor treatment from the weather conditions. Without respite the wind and the rain assaulted the belvedere for three days. And while the only patches of blue sky brightening the horizon were the sky-blue blankets in which the dressers wrapped the chilled actors after each take, everyone had the strange impression of taking part in some Arabian remake of *Wuthering Heights*, casting the most 'dangerous' of Valmonts in the role of Heathcliff.
❱ We were often forced to leave the hotel at dawn. Our endless procession of cars, trucks and trailers would rack up four to five hours daily of travel towards 'nearby' locations. Each morning, just before our arrival at the ancient mud-brick village of Tamnougalt in order to film all the exteriors of Bou Noura, the entire crew still had to brave an epic crossing of the river Draa, swollen in turn by recent storms.
❱ The striking beauty of the place fully compensated the discomfort of the trek. For the first time in three months, we had the fascinating sensation of entering both another world and another age.

BENI ABBES: From the top of the great dune, the fort Sba, was built right under our hotel's windows.

There was virtually no need to adapt the sites before cameras rolled, as nothing had changed since 1947 — whether that was 1947 B.C. or A.D., nobody could tell! Here, while Kit was pretending to be a corpse in the cemetery, under the mournful eye of a husband, ignorant of his own imminent demise, we received the first magazines commenting on the fall of the Berlin Wall — two weeks late. Suddenly, the exorbitant telephone charges of the local hotels no longer discouraged us from communicating with the outside world!

▶ The last days of our Moroccan stay were dedicated to the artificially-created night of the brothel sequence. This was shot inside the Kasbah in Ouarzazate. Some sixty prostitutes of all ages had accompanied the crew from Erfoud to help create what promised to be one of the main events of the filming. For three days, the camera followed Port from one room to another among the red shadows of this disturbing resurrection of *Sodom and Gomorrah*, led on by the hypnotic age-old rhythms of the celebrated Jajouka musicians who recorded two albums with the Rolling Stones. Before leaving the set for the last time, Bernardo spoke for everyone when he said: '*I am very sad because our paths separate here. But I'm also very happy because everything you have given us is absolutely unique. Our eyes, our ears, and our hearts will always remember you through this film.*'

ALGERIA

BENI ABBES
From December 2nd to 19th, 1989

▶ When the airplane touched down at Bechar airport, some forty Land Rovers, with their headlights already on, prepared to transport us across the desert to Beni Abbès, an immense green island surrounded by endless waves of sand. Exhausted, we travelled on, and looking up, we suddenly felt we were in a vast natural planetarium. Reaching out we could have touched the myriad of stars. At the end of the trail was the sprawling Hotel Rym which rapidly became a mirror of small town life with its chic districts and its suburbs full of spaghetti houses, a boisterous pub and a private '*rai*' disco open twenty-four hours a day.

▶ The every day tiring drives, to and from the locations, were at least over. This time the only set to be used was situated just beneath the windows of our hotel. Built for a mere 350,000 dollars, the Fort of Sba was sheltered by the great dune which dominates the old village. The weather was capricious as usual. Just when we needed the forecast of sandstorms, the wind dropped and everything was still under a cloudless blue sky. Wind machines were hijacked by the 2nd unit from the Special Effects department and put to good use.

▶ In the meantime, a select group of technicians were surrounding John Malkovich and Debra Winger behind the closed doors of the 'White Room', where Port was dying. Everyone was caught more and more in the gravity of this strange atmosphere, until the man's last sigh finally broke the tension. Then Malkovich tiptoed off the set and out of the fim. A Land Rover took him to the nearest airport.

▶ The next day, as if guided by some inner compelling need, a woman dived into a pool on the edge of a silent palm grove. When she surfaced upon Bernardo's 'cut', Kit's eyes stared at us from Debra's face. This was the last shot of 1989. A few hours later, we were catapulted to Rome, Paris and London, and were plunged into the maelstrom of last minute Christmas shopping.

.74.

With his eyes behind the viewfinder, Bertolucci is the first witness of Port's agony inside the 'White Room'.

'While shooting here, we received the news of the fall of the Berlin Wall, two weeks late.'   BERTOLUCCI on the dolly in front of the specially built fort while setting up a sequence.

BENI ABBES
From January 6th to 18th, 1990

▶ We picked up where we had left off. Here is Debra, a haggard figure against a parched backdrop, not far from the pool. Her gaze is fixed on some invisible beyond, as she faces the one-eyed 'instrument of truth' ready to photograph the slightest movements of her soul. '*Silenzio!... Motore!... Action!*' Focus on Kit, lost in her waking dream, whilst in the distance a mirage in form of a caravan enters the frame. She looks over her shoulder and hands her suitcase to the the first camel driver passing by, before accepting the 'lift' from Belqassim whom she immediately recognises as her new 'ride'.

▶ For a whole week the fifty camels of the caravan were to be our best guides to help the crew find its way through the dunes opening onto the terrifying beauty of the Grand Erg Occidental's mineral landscape. Inevitably, walkie-talkies and loudspeakers were in constant use to relay messages from one ridge to another to enable us to follow — sometimes with four cameras — the winding procession of camels. However, no doubt, the prize for devotion belonged to our team of anonymous desert-sweepers, in charge of erasing all traces of footprints before each take, in order to restore the indispensable purity to the dunes which the characters had to walk over.

▶ Not before long, under the blazing sun, and mesmerised by the light of a shimmering moon, Debra had undergone a remarkable metamorphosis. Readily forgetting her mother tongue and preferring to reply in French or in the Tuareg language, she spent most of the time on top of her favourite camel, gazing beyond the horizon and radiating a combination of energy and humour, à la Katharine Hepburn. It was as though the contact with the blue-turbaned Tuaregs had allowed Debra, and Kit, to recapture the secret of a nomad past of which they had retained a faint memory.

NIGER

AGADEZ
From January 17th to 27th, 1990

▶ After losing a whole day camped at Bechar airport caught up in futile red tape, the crew — now reduced to fifty — was ready to cross the Southern frontier of the Sahara at the Niger border. Heat and dust, beauty and extreme poverty awaited us in Agadez. This last part of our journey was to coincide with the route of the Paris-Dakar rally. Now the challenge was to complete the shoot in less than ten days. Still to come was the whole episode devoted to the forbidden liaison between Kit and Belqassim.

▶ Unresisting, Kit has allowed herself to be locked behind the closed door of the 'Mud Room' where she burns with desire at each of her Tuareg's secret visits. Without words, the two strangers continue their mysterious dialogue based solely on the use of of body language. Meanwhile, Bernardo decided to delete ten pages from the script and succeeded in reconstructing, day by day, the whole sequence of the events in order to capture the very essence of Kit's long captivity.

▶ A major surprise was in store for the last day of filming during the market scene in which Kit, dressed as an Arab, attempts to buy some milk with worthless banknotes. In a quiet corner, the young black man who was to be her new guide to the post office, was conscientiously reading his lines, when the native extras apparently missunderstood and thought that Kit's dispute with the milk vendor was a real argument. Everyone joined in and the whole set suddenly disintegrated as the crowd hurled themselves on Debra, who was virtually being lynched under our incredulous eyes. Only two of us retained presence of mind — the steadicam operator, who almost unvoluntarily kept filming, and Bernardo who called '*cut*' at the last possible moment. It was a perfect conclusion for that afternoon of January 26th, when '*cinéma-vérité*' had triumphed over fiction.

▶ In the intoxication of this unique moment, tears of joy mingled with the sadness of the abrupt end to the four months of filming. As our American actress attempted to conceal her emotion by leading the traditional applause, someone noticed that her hands, stained with the dye of the Tuaregs' blue clothes, had become exactly the same colour as her eyes.

FABIEN S. GERARD, worked as Bernardo Bertolucci's assistant on both *The Last Emperor* and *The Sheltering Sky*. Also an artist and a writer, he is the author of the shooting diary of *The Last Emperor* (*Ombres Jaunes*, Editions Cahiers di Cinéma). In 1981 he published a study on Pasolini (*Pasolini ou le Mythe de la Barbarie*, Editions de l'Université de Bruxelles).

A 'desert-sweeper' from Cinecittà erases - between takes - all human traces.

Beni Abbès: everyone mucks in to recreate an artificial sandstorm.

As soon as the clouds go, the crew moves in again to shoot a new close-up of Kit on her favourite camel.

In January the sky over the Sahara is less of a shelter than a threat, and the sand is cold as snow.

By the film's end, this American actress' intense identification with the Tuareg nomads is complete.

Overwelmed by the African crowd in Agadez, Bertolucci's family stare at the video replay of the last shot of the film — Kit's near lynching.

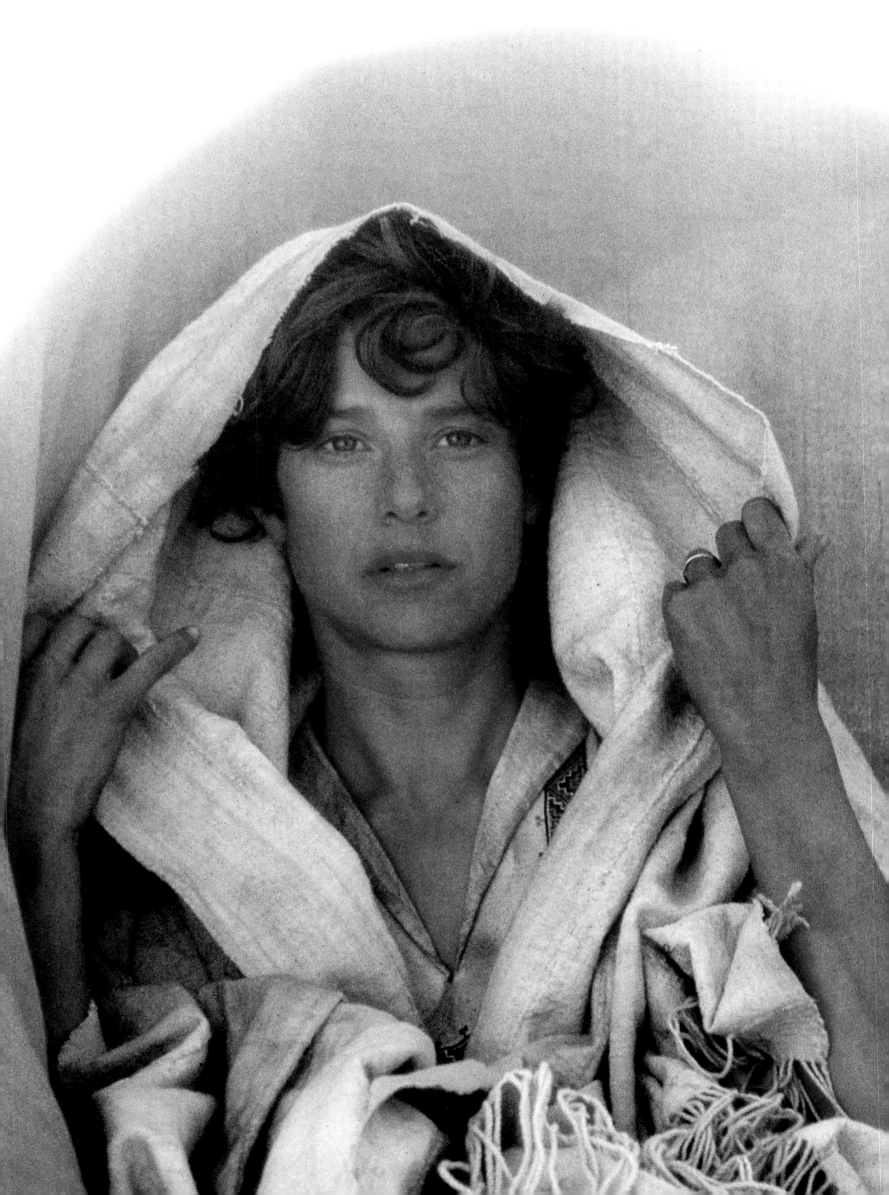

I was Blue

DEBRA WINGER IN CONVERSATION WITH PAUL BOWLES

A year after the shooting had first began, Debra Winger returned to Tangier. Her close resemblance to Jane Bowles, and her strong identification with her character Kit had left her suspended 'in character'. To regain her self-control she sought out the very man who had chartered Kit's madness and left her to disappear into the desert.

DEBRA WINGER: What will you say when people constantly ask you 'what happened to Kit?'
PAUL BOWLES: She lived happily ever after
DEBRA: No one would ever believe that.
PAUL: Well, let's see. She became the editor of an anarchist newspaper in Oran.
DEBRA: Why don't you just have her die?
PAUL: OK. She is walking along the street and sees these lovely white flowers hanging over a wall. She reaches up, pulls one off and, like the mad thing she is, puts it in her mouth and starts eating it. And, of course, it kills her.
DEBRA: So what does she do during the period before she dies?
PAUL: She says she wishes she hadn't eaten it.
DEBRA: How did you know when *The Sheltering Sky* was finished. Did it just quit on you?
PAUL: More or less. But by that time I was in a connecting room with Jane in the Grand Hotel. I was writing and she interrupted me to ask how to build a cantilever bridge. I said, *'I don't know Jane. Why do you have to know that?'* And she said, *'I can't write unless I know how it is built.'* That's when I finished the story.
DEBRA: Do you think Jane unconsciously knew she was competing with Kit?
PAUL: It upset her when she finally read about it because she thought it was an omen and that I thought she would lose her mind and go to pieces. It was impossible to explain that it had nothing to do with her, but she didn't believe it.
DEBRA: And did she believe you to be Port?
PAUL: I don't know. She said, *'It makes me very sad when I read about how Port dies.'*
DEBRA: So she felt there was a lot of her present?
PAUL: Oh, yes, she thought it was her.
DEBRA: So if Jane felt that way, I shouldn't feel so bad about all this identification with Kit?
PAUL: Where did the idea come from, in fact, that you should look like Jane?
DEBRA: The first time I saw a picture of Jane I thought it looked like me and having read *The Sheltering Sky* and Jane's works I could only picture Kit in one way. When I met Bernardo for the first time in Rome, I had my hair cut like Jane's. Bernardo responded very well. Then when I met you it seemed there was room for me to communicate with you and that room was quite possibly the space she occupied. So it became an obsession.
PAUL: Jane never made that trip. You made it for her.
DEBRA: It was a rough journey. Although I suppose you thought you treated Port a lot tougher.
PAUL: Well, that depends on which you think is worse. At least he didn't end up in a brothel.
DEBRA: Well, neither did I, but I know you would like to safely stow me away in one.
PAUL: It's not my fault if Kit went mad.
DEBRA: Well, allow me to correct you, maybe not mad but you sent me round the bend and off the track.
PAUL: I'm never quite sure when you cease being normal.

DEBRA WINGER and PAUL BOWLES on the set of *The Sheltering Sky*, Tangier, October 1989.

DEBRA WINGER :
*'I really do think I found
where I belong.'*

DEBRA: You don't think I'm crazy, do you?

PAUL: I don't think you are crazy. If you are Kit, you are. That's the way it goes.

DEBRA: OK, now for the final question. Who do you think I am?

PAUL: Oh, I thought you were thinking about your life as Kit.

DEBRA: It's the same thing. It's not possible to put your life aside while you're working. It just hangs around all the time waiting to be noticed.

PAUL: To be noticed and petted.

DEBRA: Mine, in this case, was kicked a few times as opposed to being petted. I mean you sent me to places you wouldn't be seen dead in. How dare you do that?

PAUL: Well, I'm sorry. I didn't really have any concept of the places you would be sent.

DEBRA: I felt very at home with the Tuaregs. They were nice people. I expected to experience some kind of terror, but the terror went. Maybe I took Port's strength after he died.

PAUL: A strength born of faith in yourself I suppose.

DEBRA: The Tuaregs were the first people I have ever met who have the same hands and toes as me. So I really do think I have found where I belong.

PAUL: Your ethnic roots?

DEBRA: Yes, although it was strange to wear indigo fabric which dyes your skin. I was blue. The painful binding on my chest even coloured my breasts, which was a very unusual sight. But the pain was not as great as when Port and I had to make love on the rocks.

PAUL: What, up there in full sight of the public?

DEBRA: No, in full sight of the desert. I thought it was very violent. Bernardo thought I meant the emotional content of the scene until I explained that I had various jagged rocks in my back. But it was painful as well because it was Port and Kit trying to communicate. To agree to do anything was impossible.

PAUL: So, how did you feel about Port's death?

DEBRA: After his death I was so happy, so free. I felt like I had taken charge. I felt Kit was still carrying on all Port's stuff but I felt lighter with no responsibility to him. The role suddenly changed when he died and John Malkovich — Port — disappears, you know, he went home and I was there and so the story became reality. It was very uncomfortable, in the beginning, to play such a sexually, verbally and physically suppressed person.

PAUL: Generally one suppresses because of others.

DEBRA: In this case one other. Port and Kit always suppressed things when they shouldn't have and when they should have shut their mouths, they didn't. I felt very neurotic at the beginning of the filming in Tangier and would find the energy would come out in other ways — nervous energy. When you're writing does it come out? Do you assume the energy of your characters?

PAUL: No, I try to keep them at arm's length, at least from everything. A writer is not supposed to feel, he is supposed to imagine.

DEBRA: Maybe that's why I always feel so neurotic. There were very provocative questions demanded of a girl left alone out in the desert. These questions were not easy. Don't you think it's the responsability of the person asking the questions to provide answers to them?

PAUL: Well, maybe he should know the answers but he doesn't have to divulge them. It's easier to find the answer than the question.

DEBRA: I'm absolutely lost looking for the question. There is no redemption. So am I lost?

Edited by CATHERINE MACKENZIE

JANE BOWLES, 1937.

DEBRA WINGER, 1989.

DEBRA WINGER to PAUL BOWLES: *'I am absolutely lost looking for the question? Is there no redemption — any answer? So am I lost?'*

Life as a Road Movie

BY MARK PEPLOE

I was born in Africa outside Nairobi. One of my first memories was of our journey up the Nile to Cairo. We arrived in Italy when I was three, in England when I was five. It was 1948. London was still full of bombsites. I remember playing hide and seek in the ruins.

MARK PEPLOE and CLARE PEPLOE during the shooting of THE LAST EMPEROR, BEIJING, 1986.

▶ The first film I ever saw was *Scott of the Antartic*, the story of the explorer's suicidal journey to the North pole. The second, which was a documentary in colour, also took place amongst ice and snow.

▶ There was a long gap after this until one Sunday, when I was about eight, my father startled me by asking if I wanted to go to the cinema. He had never done this before. We took a taxi to a place called Leicester Square and arrived at the Empire Cinema. In those days it was decorated with zebra skins and elephant tusks.

I can still remember the *'madeleine-like sensation'* I felt as *King Solomon's Mines* began and the sounds of Africa took me back to my already forgotten beginning. Cinema, travel, and identity have seemed inextricably linked for me ever since.

▶ One day, when I was seventeen, I took a train out of Victoria station and kept on going until I got to Kathmandu.

▶ I first went to Morocco, with my sister, in 1961. I will never forget the afternoon we crossed the Atlas Mountains and saw the landscape around Ouarzazate for the first time. Watching the desert through the windscreen of a moving car made me a passenger for life.

▶ The roads at that time were all still dirt roads. By the side of one of them, we chanced upon a solitary sign — pointing into the desert — which said *Lawrence of Arabia*. We followed it and arrived in the midst of a huge battle scene. It was the first movie set I had ever been on.

▶ I read *The Sheltering Sky* in 1964 and felt an extraordinary sense of recognition about the world it describes. Five years later, when I gave up documentary film-making and decided to write a screenplay, this was the novel I wanted to adapt. But Robert Aldrich owned the rights and wouldn't part with them. So I wrote another story called *The Passenger* which begins with a man who dies in the desert and another man who takes his identity and inherits his journey. Life as a road movie.

▶ I went back to Morocco in 1968, 1969 and 1972. Each journey was part of a love story, ending or beginning.

▶ Fifteen years later, in China, Bernardo began mentioning a book he had been offered by William Aldrich, Robert's son, called *The Sheltering Sky*. I tried to say very little. Shortly afterwards he asked if I wanted to work on the screenplay. There was something dream-like about the way this story had come back into my life, and two years later, about finding myself driving again through the landscape of North Africa and sleeping again in some of the same long-forgotten hotel rooms I had been in years before.

▶ The problem of adapting Bowles' novel into a screenplay for Bertolucci, of being a kind of cinematic go-between for two such particular artists (as well as between them and Warner Bros) proved as difficult as I had imagined; frustrating and fascinating at the same time. Some tasks may be impossible, but we live our lives for the chance.

▶ In the script I tried to hold on to some simple ideas. 1947. The last month in a ten-year-old marriage. A huge feeling of suspense. An existential love story with the structure of a Hitchcock thriller. Three characters, then two, then only one....

▶ It is easy to describe the story of *The Sheltering Sky* and make it sound utterly

JACK NICHOLSON in ANTONIONI's *THE PASSENGER* ,1973. *'I wrote a story which begins with a man who dies in the desert and another man who takes his identity and inherits his journey.'*

LAWRENCE OF ARABIA, David Lean, 1961. *'We chanced upon a solitary sign - pointing into the desert - which said 'Lawrence of Arabia'. It was the first movie set I had ever been on.'*

depressing, a tale without hope. But, personally, I had never felt this about it and I would often ask myself why.

▶ There is nothing in the world forcing Port and Kit to be together except themselves. And while the current of the story moves inexorably against them, their struggle to exist as a couple becomes mysteriously heroic, as if these two unlikely and imperfect people stood for everyone else.

▶ The nightmare that lurks behind *The Sheltering Sky* is that life may have no meaning, that the sky protects us from nothing except permanent night.

▶ But there is a paradox in Bowles' nihilism. Port dies and his death is terrible. Yet the story goes on, almost by that fact alone extracting meaning from Kit's descent into nothingness.

▶ What you see in the desert sky at night is the awesome clock of the universe which stops for no death. In outer space permanent night exists at the same time as eternal day.

Screenwriter MARK PEPLOE, who co-wrote the Academy Award-winning script of *The Last Emperor*, spent four years working in documentary television before turning to screenwriting in 1969. He has written for Joseph Losey, Jonathan Demme, André Konchalovsky, Jacques Demy, René Clément, Jacques Deray, Clare Peploe and has had a long association with Michelangelo Antonioni for whom he wrote the original screenplay of *The Passenger*. As writer-director, he is presently preparing a psychological thriller *Afraid of the Dark*.

Thirty Years in the Making

BY WILLIAM ALDRICH

Paul Bowles' *The Sheltering Sky* **was published in 1949. My father, the director Robert Aldrich, first optioned the book and then in 1964 bought it outright. For over twenty years it was his private dream to see** *The Sheltering Sky* **filmed as he had first read it on the page and then as he imagined it so vividly.**

▶ Timing is everything. Before Dad became obsessed with the story, Bowles' novel had been available for a number of years. But in the early fifties, filmgoers were thought to be unlikely to warm up to the often scarifying but beautiful story of a couple striving to find each other and, in the process, losing everything. Some readers in Hollywood were frightened by the implied criticism of capitalism — what else, after all, could so tarnish two beautiful talented people? Remember, this was mid-McCarthy time.

▶ Later when Dwight Eisenhower was elected, after McCarthy's decline, the world turned smoothly on its axis. Suburbia grew. Children were raised peacefully without drugs, without their fists clenched in the air, without the Pill. These were the years of *Pillow Talk*, eons away from *Last Tango in Paris*.

▶ Every time Dad made a deal for a picture — *What Happened To Baby Jane?*, *The Dirty Dozen*, *The Longest Yard*, — he carried *The Sheltering Sky* with him. At one point he himself wrote a first draft of the picture, then another, but he found, as I did many years later, that the book was its own best advertisement.

▶ By the mid-sixties and into the early seventies, after I had worked my way through my father's company — summertime go-fer, third assistant director, coordinator of post-production, assistant and then associate producer — Dad's joy in *The Sheltering Sky* was tempered a little by disappointment. His primary reputation rested on what are called 'action pictures', and studios thought him too rough-edged for a picture as delicate as this one would have to be.

▶ Dad's dream, tarnished a bit, lived still. At one point having been offered a sizeable amount for the rights to the book, he and I had a long and thoughtful conversation. My suggestion — having produced *Who is Killing the Great Chief of Europe?* (1978), and *All the Marbles* (1981) on my own — was that I could produce the film, hire a director whose vision of the material matched our own, and The Aldrich Company could, therefore, retain all interest in and affection for the piece.

▶ It was a month before Dad actually made a decision. What I didn't know, and I am not sure he did either, was that his own strength was ebbing. To go on a four to six month regimen of physical training, as was his custom before filming any picture began, must now have been beyond him. Although he desperately wanted no one else to direct the picture, finally he agreed that my idea had merit.

▶ But in 1983, before we could swing into action, my father died. *The Sheltering Sky* was part of his legacy to The Aldrich Company. Seeing it made became one of my most energizing goals.

▶ What I found as president of The Aldrich Company was that no reader, and not one writer, was frightened by the project. Often people asked to be allowed to work on the film for free. What had to be done before thinking about a writer, however, was to find a director who could film the book's vision. For nearly two years I met with American film-makers. But in all that time, none seemed to feel, as I did, that the interior lives of Port Moresby and his wife Kit mattered as much as the wide-screen action and suspense of their story. I began to think that perhaps a European sensibility would be more in tune with the material.

▶ As it happened, in 1985, Bernardo Bertolucci was coming to California to try to secure financing for *The Last Emperor*. From our first hours together, I felt certain that Bernardo was probably the only director who could do justice to

ROBERT ALDRICH directing PIER ANGELI in *SODOM AND GOMORRAH*, 1961.

WILLIAM ALDRICH with PAUL BOWLES, TANGIER, 1989.

The Sheltering Sky. He had read the book years before and remembered it with astonishing clarity and had an instinctive point of view with which I agreed. I knew that he could bring both stories to the screen — a deeply felt, very strange, eerily eternal romance, as well as the story of young rootless Americans out for a lark in North Africa, a lark that turns tragic and desperate and which, for both of them, holds mystery and enchantment. Warners Bros agreed.

▶ Bernardo and I met with several writers in Los Angeles, and I spoke with others from abroad. Then Bernardo told me that the writer of *The Last Emperor*, Mark Peploe, was coming to Los Angeles. Would I read his screenplay for that film, as well as two others Mark had written? I did, and I was as convinced as Bernardo that Mark was our man.

▶ When *The Last Emperor* became a 'go' project, none of us could have imagined how long and tortuous it would be to make. But the moment in October of 1989 that I stepped on the set of *The Sheltering Sky* in Tangier, I knew our long wait had borne spectacular fruit.

▶ The setting was the hotel room that Port and Kit first take when they arrive in North Africa. As Paul Bowles had written so long ago, '*the high, narrow room with its beamed ceiling, the huge apathetic designs stencilled in indifferent colours around the walls, the closed window of red and orange glass ...*' — all of this greeted me as though it were a dream I had tossed and turned over night after night, finally to wake and see clearly — and accurately — for the first time.

▶ What Paul Bowles had helped us imagine was precisely what Bernardo presented to us as reality. Later when filming for that day ended, I returned to my hotel room totally exhilarated. My wife Barbara and I chose to dine in that night because, understanding how close we all were now to the accomplishment of a vision that had lasted three decades, my joy had suddenly turned into exhaustion. The energy and devotion to such an undertaking for such a long period had simply drained me.

▶ When finally I dozed off, to be wakened at four thirty by the regular call of an imam, I felt utterly safe and at ease under 'the sheltering sky'.

Being the son of the film director Robert Aldrich, **executive-producer WILLIAM ALDRICH**, grew up around films. He went to the University of Southern California to study law and business, but later changed to a film course, much against the advice of his father who considered a degree in law and business to be much more useful. In 1967 Aldrich left university to join his father's company, subsequently working as a producer.

Writing with Light

BY VITTORIO STORARO

VITTORIO STORARO with his camera operator ENRICO UMETELLI.

'The subconscious effect of the colours upon audience will either help tell the story or hinder it.'

▶ The word 'photography' literally means 'writing with light', and what I write with light are cinematic stories. Over the years, studying the physiological effects that colours of light have upon the people who see them, I have developed my own ideology of light in terms of film narrative. My normal pattern is to apply my ideology to the film, but with *The Sheltering Sky* it was different. I had just come from shooting Warren Beatty's *Dick Tracy*, which had a very strong visual style. It was difficult to shake. Normally I have a bit of reprieve to clear my head between assignments of this magnitude, but this time I had to begin *The Sheltering Sky* almost immediately. As I read Paul Bowles' novel, I became increasingly aware that he had already written strong indications of the light into virtually every scene. My ideology would certainly be employed in the colouring, the lighting and the photography, but it would come from within the story and not be superimposed upon it. The book became my bible.

▶ *The Sheltering Sky* is a recounting of a journey in the lives of two characters, Port and Kit. The first part of the tale belongs to Port, the dominant one, the sun. The second part of the story belongs to Kit, the more submissive of the two, the moon. The fact that the story is set in Africa makes those two natural symbols of light, the sun and the moon, all the more important and the more difficult to ignore. At the beginning of the film it is day and Port is at the height of his powers. Kit is almost invisible, much the way the moon is when in the sky at the same time as the sun. But as Port sickens, the sun is going down. When he dies, it is nightfall. As Kit is left alone in an alien land, her moon begins to rise. It becomes her story. The journey of their lives parallels the journey of the sun and the moon.

▶ The sun, of course, represents the hot colours, the masculine colours, the reds and the oranges. The moon reflects the cooler colours, the indigos and the blues. Perhaps it is significant that as a couple, they only come to terms with their relationship as they sit and watch the sun go down, over a vast plain, at the time when the two lights pass each other. It is only then that they find their truth.

▶ The subconscious effect of the colours upon an audience in a movie house will either help tell the story or hinder it. Light is a physical thing. It enters the eyes, and therefore the brains of the people who are looking at it. The wavelengths of the various tones impart particular psychological signals, which the audience absorbs. It alters their blood pressure, their metabolism, their physical input. It is my work to tell the story of the script, in this case the story of Port and Kit, carefully employing my understanding of these principles, while writing with light.

Cinematographer VITTORIO STORARO, started out in 1964 as the youngest first assistant cameraman and camera operator in the Italian film industry. His collaboration with Bertolucci has produced films such as *The Conformist*, *Last Tango in Paris* and *1900*. In 1979 Francis Coppola's *Apocalypse Now* brought Storaro his first Oscar for 'Best Photography'. Two other Oscars followed, in 1981 for Warren Beatty's *Reds*, and in 1987 for *The Last Emperor*. Other films include *One from the Heart*, *Wagner*, *Tucker*, Coppola's segment of *New York Stories*, *Imago Urbis* (a 15-part TV series on Roman culture) and *Dick Tracy*.

1001 Ways to Tie a Turban

BY JAMES ACHESON

JAMES ACHESON with the Tuareg family of Belqassim.

'Instead of just making a lot of new clothes, I thought it was worth trying to find old authhentic djellabahs and bournouses.'

▶ This film is about the journey of two stylish but not very rich Americans through North Africa. Basically our job is to support the actors in the characterization of their part through their clothes. Since we know that Kit and Port have travelled extensively in Europe and Central America, the first point was occasionally to hint at their past by precise choices of shapes and fabrics. That's why their garments are never typically 'forties' New York' but often European. The second point was the practical side of it. Being 'Western nomads', Port and Kit's dresses had to be primarily lightweight travelling clothes — linen, cotton and rayon. Hopefully the filmgoer would never notice such details, unless he is some kind of detective!

▶ But during their journey toward the Sahara, the characters meet a completely different culture. That was the 'epic' aspect of the film, which meant that, some days, we had to dress hundreds of native extras. Instead of just making a lot of new clothes, I thought it was worth trying to find old authentic djellabahs and burnouses. In order to collect such original pieces, we made two expeditions to the Moroccan countryside. Each village's headman organized a kind of jumble sale on the square where we bought and traded. Most of the people were very happy to get rid of their worn out djellabah in return for a brand new one! We had to disinfect and dye them and then cut them up and remake them to get exactly what we wanted. In the country brothel costumes, for instance, we mixed Algerian and Moroccan themes and shapes.

▶ We had very interesting newsreel footage of nomadic life in the forties for the Tuaregs' costumes. What fascinated me was the actual weight of the fabrics and the way they moved on their bodies. It was important to use the original indigo dyed fabric to obtain that special irridescent quality. The last part of the film was more romantic and strangely dreamlike, so we were able to make some more unusual choices in terms of colours and textures.

▶ The point is to try to evoke the essence of the period and the culture you are dealing with. Every film is a unique opportunity to enter a new world. Before working in North Africa, I didn't know that a turban could be tied in so many different ways to reflect the character of the person who is wearing it. I was full of admiration for our local assistants who would sometimes tie a turban again half a dozen times just to get it right for the face of the extra. It strangely reminded me of another Italian maestro, Visconti, who used to say that many details you don't notice individually go to make the richness of the whole frame. That's the game we are in.

Costume designer JAMES ACHESON, won an Oscar for his work on *The Last Emperor* in 1988 and again collected the award the following year for Steven Frears' *Dangerous Liaisons.* He first trained in theatre design and later worked for BBC Television and for a Spanish circus as a stage manager. For the last twelve years he has dedicated his activity to cinema designing the costumes for *Bullshot, Highlander* and Terry Gilliam's *Time Bandits, The Meaning of Life* and *Brazil.*

We Slept beneath the Stars

BY GIANNI SILVESTRI

GIANNI SILVESTRI on the bastion of the fort built in Beni Abbès. *'The red walls of the fort curiously recalled the walls of the Forbidden City in* The Last Emperor.*'*

TAMNOUGALT. *'These locations had such an impact on all of us as to leave no doubt. Those had to be the stations in the hallucinating journey of Port and Kit.'*

◗ The first location scouting was carried out over the space of four months with Ferdinando Scarfiotti — Oscar winner for *The Last Emperor* — who at the time was designated as the production designer of *The Sheltering Sky*. During the final stage of preparation, Ferdinando was struck by hepatitis, so he asked me to continue the work as he had laid it out. Obviously, many things were to change, but we always kept in touch, agreeing even at great distances.

◗ We started scouting in Niger, the last place to be seen in the chronology of the film. There we found a fascinating building in Agadez in a 'barbaric-baroque' style. It was called the Baker's House, and was chosen to represent Belqassim's home. We just added on the roof the 'Mud Room' in which Kit is enclosed. Unlike the cell described in the book, it is surrounded by courtyards full of life and illuminated by the bright African sky.

◗ Our first encounter with the dunes was north of Agadez. We slept beneath the stars. From there we went up to Algeria, to Djanet, where the desert became a surreal landscape studded with tower-like rocks that jut up from the sand. I still deeply regret that at the last moment we had to abandon this site because of budget constraints.

◗ At Beni Abbès, on the edge of the Algerian Sahara, we found the ideal place to build the Fort of Sba, on a rocky plateau emerging from the dunes. The red walls of a fort seen earlier at Guelmin were to determine the colour for our construction. Curiously it recalled the walls of the Forbidden City in *The Last Emperor*, or, for that matter, the farm in *1900*.

◗ For Port's agony we created, in the interior of the 'White Room', an atmosphere of enclosing space that is somehow obsessive. From this we got the idea for the type of corridor-infirmary, outside which the legionnaires play soccer in a courtyard that was almost Mediterranean. It was reminiscent of some places in Oran or Nice.

◗ Oran seemed right for the port city at the beginning of the story, because it had remained miraculously intact for forty years. However, the usual logistical motives forced us to choose Tangier, which required some transformations. There, Scarfiotti had fallen in love with an immense metal crane, abandoned on a pier. That was enough to create the post-war 'mood' in the opening sequence of the film.

◗ As we went south into Morocco, our impressions became ever stronger, to the point of disorientation. Which were the real places described by Paul Bowles? Many times we spoke to the author about it, who evaded any indication of the true sites. Soon enough, Tinheris, Gla Gla and Tamnougalt had such an impact on all of us as to leave no doubt. Those had to be the 'stations' in the hallucinating journey of Port and Kit.

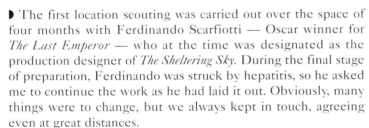

Production designer GIANNI SILVESTRI studied as a painter and an architet at the University of Rome. He started his career as a set dresser on Patroni Griffi's *One Evening at Dinner*. He created the design for several stage productions. He began his collaboration with Bernardo Bertolucci on *1900* and designed for him *La Luna,* and *The Tragedy of a Ridiculous Man,* and was the art director on *The Last Emperor*. Other credits include *A Simple Heart, Honeymoon for Three* , Costa Grava's *Anna K.* and Peter Bogdanovich's *Daisy Miller*.

Every Cut Has to Heal

BY GABRIELLA CRISTIANI

GABRIELLA CRISTIANI editing the film on laser disk CMX 6000.

GABRIELLA CRISTIANI (left) directing a sequence of her documentary on *The Sheltering Sky.*

▶ The editing room has been compared to an operating theatre. It is true that at times the pieces of film lying on the floor seem to be floating in blood. The blood, of course, is that of the director who often thinks of the editor as his personal executioner. In reality, our work has as much to do with psychology as it does with technology. With someone like Bernardo, you have got to impose a certain discipline if you are going to get him to face facts. I mean, often, while watching the rushes, you know that certain sequences are never going to find their way into the final version. I am convinced that Bernardo knows, but he needs a little time to get used to it. It is almost as if every cut is made in his own flesh, and it needs to heal.

▶ He is incorrigible. For someone like him, the pleasure of shooting has grown over the years — more than the torment of having to cut things later. In the case of *The Sheltering Sky*, we began with a first version of the film which was four hours long and closely followed the plot of the book. Instead, the definitive version ended up two hours and twenty minutes long, after we rewrote the story for the last time. After all, I guess, I learned my trade with the great Kim Arcalli — the only editor who was ever credited as co-scriptwriter.

▶ We were editing the film with the new laser technology, which we were experimenting with for the first time, we were able to try out all the combinations in record time. When Bernardo realizes that the story 'works', that it flows smoothly across the screen, he is as happy as a baby to see that he has done it again.

▶ Almost by accident, some of the scenes which were cut out were inserted in the documentary 'on the making', which I had the honour and the pleasure to shoot. In the documentary we also had to abandon some beautiful footage, but oddly enough, since I didn't have to worry about 'hurting' anyone else, I found it much easier to cut my own material. As I was the director of the documentary it had been easier to ignore myself. The editing room of the documentary was literally opposite where I was editing the feature film. It seemed that people found it amusing to see me running, for months on end, from one editing room to another. As soon as there was a break, I would leave Bernardo in the company of Port and Kit behind one door, and then meet up with them again behind the next. In the documentary Bernardo would be with John Malkovich and Debra Winger in their dressing gowns — all of them 'lost' in the thousand little stories that make up the life of a film set. I found it very exciting working on two films simultaneously. Useful, too, because the two films are connected and communicate with each other. One would help me to find the solution I was seeking in the other, and vice versa.

Editor GABRIELLA CRISTIANI, winner of an Oscar for 'Best Editing' for *The Last Emperor*, began her career as the first assistant editor of the renowned Kim Arcalli on *Last Tango in Paris* and *1900*, and since then has edited over thirty films. Among her credits she includes *La Luna, The Tragedy of a Ridiculous Man, Couples and Robbers, Samson and Dalilah, High Season*, and *Francesco d'Assisi*. She has directed a documentary on the making of *The Sheltering Sky* and is currently completing a documentary on cinematographer Vittorio Storaro entitled *Writing with Light*.

Desert Tones

BY RYUICHI SAKAMOTO AND RICHARD HOROWITZ

RYUICHI SAKAMOTO

RICHARD HOROWITZ

RYUICHI SAKAMOTO

▶ As soon as I knew about Bertolucci's *The Sheltering Sky*, I started reading Bowles' novel. I realized that it was most unlikely that I would gane an opportunituy to play a Japanese in this film, just as I played Mr Amakasu in *The Last Emperor*. Therefore, my only chance to be involved was to hope Bertolucci would call me as a composer instead of an actor.

▶ Just as Bernardo had asked me to mix ancient Chinese music with Western music in *The Last Emperor*, he asked me again in this movie to operate a delicate fusion with opposite sensibilities. In *The Sheltering Sky* for example, in the last part of the desert scenes I adapted the 'rai' sounds of the eighties previously chosen by Bernardo, by using original Arab drums and violins instead of the synthetizer, in order to fit into the original musical background.

▶ I also listened Paul Bowles' music. I think it is quite good — a lot of Ravel, bits of Stravinsky. He wasn't a writer who wanted to compose but a real composer who was able to write as well and became a novelist. As Port, in the film, is a composer too, the idea was to write some kind of music that the protagonist could write himself.

▶ Together with Bertolucci we decided to use one single theme with several variations throughout the whole film. It is called 'poison' because Port and Kit's relationship appears full of painful venom. As the story progresses, the variations work nostalgically, each one on a different level. At the end, when Kit comes back to the Grand Hotel, you feel her body is in Tangier but not her mind. The music is the sound of her mind.

RICHARD HOROWITZ

▶ In 1969 I read *The Sheltering Sky* in Paris and made my first trip to Morocco. Two years later I returned to study, in more detail, Arabic music which has had a lasting influence on my composition. Not long after having seen *Last Tango in Paris*, in 1974, Bryon Gysin told me to go and see Paul Bowles in Tangier. His work, friendship and understanding have continued to be a deep source of inspiration ever since.

▶ While Bertolucci was filming on location, I recorded over one hundred musicians on my digital recorder and worked in an improvised recording studio in a hotel room on various keyboards in search of the appropriate 'primitive rhythms' to accompany Kit and Port's journey towards the south. Port becomes a composer in the screenplay and the large amount of local music in the soundtrack of the film is a reflection of his particular interest in world music. It was also a main concern of Paul's in the forties, before writing *The Sheltering Sky*.

Composer and record producer RYUICHI SAKAMOTO won an Oscar for the soundtrack of *The Last Emperor*. He studied music composition at the University of Tokyo and has since released several albums including *Thousand Knives, B-2 Unit, Left Hand Dream Field Work* (with Thomas Dolby), *Neo Geo and Beauty*. As an actor he has performed in *Merry Christmas Mr Lawrence* and *The Last Emperor*.

Composer and North African music expert RICHARD HOROWITZ was recommended by Paul Bowles, in 1981, to the American Academy of Arts for the Goddard Libberson Composition Award. He lived in Morocco from 1974 to 1979 and has collaborated with Susan Deihim since 1981. His recordings include *Eros in Arabia, Ibn Sabbah: Ghost of the Assassination* and *X-Isle Isle-X*.

The Right Moment

BY JEREMY THOMAS

JEREMY THOMAS.

'Like the palaces in The Last Emperor, *the exotic locations of* The Sheltering Sky *are a feast for the eye'.*

▶ Ten years ago, Nicolas Roeg told me he wanted to make a film of *The Sheltering Sky*. I loved the novel and made an offer to Robert Aldrich who owned the rights, but he was not at all interested as he was still keen to make the film himself. A few years later Bernardo was offered *The Sheltering Sky*, and he asked me if I'd produce it. I then discovered that Mark Peploe had had a long 'affair' with the book, and this seemed to be the completion of a circle, the three of us reunited on this project so soon after *The Last Emperor*. A strange and happy coincidence.

▶ The nine Oscars we won in 1988 obviously made everybody very confident, and this helped us to make *The Sheltering Sky* in the same independent, freewheeling way that we made *The Last Emperor*. On the whole, filming in North Africa was prove more difficult than in China. To get the various permissions to set the project in motion was not at all easy in China, but in terms of physical production the logistic problems on *The Sheltering Sky* were far harder.

▶ The film is a kind of 'road movie', so we had to prepare ahead all the time to get the crew and equipment to a number of distant locations. We shot in three different countries, each one with very different problems. For example authorizations for our charter planes to land or take off were often delayed, and this lost us a lot of time. We also had to build a large French Legion fort in the middle of the sand dunes, entirely out of material which we brought with us. The filming ended in Niger, which is one of the poorest countries in the world; no film had been shot there before, and we had to completely organize our own infrastructure.

▶ Like the palaces in *The Last Emperor*, the exotic locations of *The Sheltering Sky* are a feast for the eye, but the subject is very different — much more intimate. A profound love story and a haunting tale that is impossible to put down once you start reading it — and that of course is instantly attractive for a film. Paul Bowles had to wait a long time to see his book on the screen, but the recent worldwilde interest in this project seems proof that the right moment to do it had finally arrived. Bertolucci and Bowles — a perfect combination.

Producer JEREMY THOMAS, was born in London in 1949, son of a film-making family. He started working as an editor in 1974 on Philippe Mora's *Brother Can you Spare a Dime?* and then travelled to Australia to produce his first film, *Mad Dog Morgan*. Thomas went on to produce films made by highly individual directors such as Nicolas Roeg (*Bad Timing, Eureka, Insignificance*), Nagisa Oshima (*Merry Christmas Mr Lawrence*), Stephen Frears (*The Hit*), Jerzy Skolimowski (The Shout), Julien Temple (*The Great Rock 'n' Roll Swindle*), Karel Reisz (*Everybody Wins*) and Bernardo Bertolucci (*The Last Emperor*). Since shooting was completed on *The Sheltering Sky*, Thomas has been working on a number of projects, most notably the film of William Burrough's novel, *The Naked Lunch*, directed by David Cronenberg.

JEREMY THOMAS Presents
a BERNARDO BRETOLUCCI film
DEBRA WINGER and JOHN MALKOVICH in THE SHELTERING SKY
Presented in association with THE ALDRICH GROUP
starring CAMPBELL SCOTT, JILL BENNETT, TIMOTHY SPALL
AMINA ANNABI, SOTIGUI KOYATE
PHILIPPE MORIER-GENOUD, BEN SMAIL
and introducing ERIC VU-AN as "BELQASSIM"
2nd Unit Director/Director's Consultant FERNAND MOSZKOVICZ
Casting by JULIET TAYLOR Financial Controller RON SWINBURNE
Art Director ANDREW SANDERS Production Designer GIANNI SILVESTRI

Costume Designer JAMES ACHESON Editor GABRIELLA CRISTIANI
Cinematography by VITTORIO STORARO AIC-ASC (Technicolor-Technovision)
Music by RYUICHI SAKAMOTO
Additional African Music by RICHARD HOROWITZ
Music Supervisor RAY WILLIAMS
Production Supervisor DENISE O'DELL
Executive Producer WILLIAM ALDRICH
based on the book by PAUL BOWLES
Screenplay MARK PEPLOE with BERNARDO BERTOLUCCI
Producer JEREMY THOMAS
Director BERNARDO BERTOLUCCI